M

746.432

Carro.C

Knitting Sweaters from the Top Down

Fabulous Seamless Patterns to Suit Your Style

Knitting Sweaters

from the
Top Down

**Fabulous
Seamless
Patterns
to Suit
Your
Style**

Cathy
Carron

LARK BOOKS
A Division of
Sterling Publishing Co., Inc.
New York

Editor:

Joanne O'Sullivan

Art Director:

Megan Kirby

Cover Designer:

Barbara Zaretsky

Associate Editor:

Susan Kieffer

Associate Art Director:

Shannon Yokeley

Art Production Assistant:

Jeff Hamilton

Editorial Assistance:

Delores Gosnell

Illustrator:

Orrin Lundgren

Photographer:

Stewart O'Shields

Library of Congress Cataloging-in-Publication Data

Carron, Cathy.
  Knitting sweaters from the top down: fabulous seamless patterns to suit
your style / by Cathy Carron. -- 1st ed.
      p. cm.
   Includes index.
   ISBN 1-57990-858-6 (hardcover)
   1. Sweaters. 2. Knitting--Patterns. I. Title.
   TT825.C233 2007
   746.43'20432--dc22
                                                        2006023939

10 9 8 7 6 5 4 3 2 1

First Edition

Published by Lark Books, A Division of
Sterling Publishing Co., Inc.
387 Park Avenue South, New York, N.Y. 10016

Text © 2007, Cathy Carron
Photography © 2007, Lark Books
Illustrations © 2007, Lark Books

Distributed in Canada by Sterling Publishing,
c/o Canadian Manda Group, 165 Dufferin Street
Toronto, Ontario, Canada M6K 3H6

Distributed in the United Kingdom by GMC Distribution Services,
Castle Place, 166 High Street, Lewes, East Sussex, England BN7 1XU

Distributed in Australia by Capricorn Link (Australia) Pty Ltd.,
P.O. Box 704, Windsor, NSW 2756 Australia

If you have questions or comments about this book, please contact:
Lark Books
67 Broadway
Asheville, NC 28801
(828) 253-0467

Manufactured in China

ISBN 13: 978-1-57990-858-4
ISBN 10: 1-57990-858-6

For information about custom editions, special sales, premium and corporate purchases, please contact
Sterling Special Sales Department at 800-805-5489 or specialsales@sterlingpub.com.

For Emma and Lydia

Contents

Introduction

I made my first sweater when I was ten years old. Its handmade appearance, while charming in its own way, was not quite the professional look I was after, and I soon found myself at knitting lessons with a neighborhood expert who taught me the finer points of making buttonholes, weaving in yarn ends, and sewing seams. Although this knowledge led to sweaters with a more "finished" look, I found the process arduous. Maybe that's why the idea of top-down knitting—making a sweater in one piece with no seams—was so appealing when I stumbled upon it years later. Having given it a try, I now can't imagine making a sweater any other way. It made a lot of sense to me, and I'm sure it will to you, too.

This book is an exploration in knitting a sweater from the top down. You will not only learn to tackle and use the technique (not as difficut as it might appear), but you will also learn how to design your own fabulous and unique creations: how to add collar and cuff details, and make and shape the body and sleeves of the garment to your liking.

No other hand knitting methodology comes close in enjoyment and results to the top-down technique. It is truly a *holistic* way to create a knitted structure. The emphasis is on the whole garment and the interdependence of its parts rather than the separate bits. You begin small at the neckline and "grow" a complete structure right before your eyes. The benefits of using the top-down technique are numerous:

- Altering and shaping the garment are easier to achieve than with traditional piecemeal knitting. You can make adjustments along the way from the top downward without having to tear the whole sweater apart.

- Finishing is minimized: if you don't always end your rows perfectly, fit sleeve and body pieces together exactly, or have the skills of a couture-house assistant, you'll still be able to create a perfect sweater.

- No more patterns! Once you've got the basic concept down, yoke increases (which form the body and sleeves) are regular and predictable. You can "see" where you are in the process without having to read a pattern each step of the way.

To get you started, I'll show you how to read a typical top-down pattern. It's not difficult, but it does differ a bit from usual patterns. I'll cover designing a sweater and customizing your designs, from making style choices to adding elements such as collars, cuffs, and closures. You'll find that there are infinite combinations, limited only by your imagination. Then it's on to the math part of top-down knitting (which you can skip completely if you just want to follow the patterns). A section on choosing your yarn and needles rounds out the introduction to this technique, and then you're ready for the patterns! There's something for everyone—a range of styles, colors, and yarns. If you prefer to design your own sweater, I've also included 'basic' cardigan and pullover patterns in eight yarn gauges so that you'll have more freedom in choosing the yarn you want, too.

Once you've knitted your first top-down sweater, there's a good chance that you'll never want to go back to piecemeal knitting. The top-down technique will remind you of the real joy of knitting—the clickin' 'n' clackin' rhythm of the needles and the satisfaction of creating a garment that expresses your style. Before you know it, you'll be knitting, as they say "without a wire"—pattern-free.

Getting Started

This section is aimed primarily at beginners, so if you're already experienced with top-down knitting, you may want to skip ahead to the patterns. First off, the language of top-down knitting differs a little, so you'll want to get used to what might be new abbreviations for you in the list below; a more comprehensive abbreviations list is on page 127.

ABBREVIATIONS

cn	circular needle
dpn	double-pointed needle
B&F	back and forth
BO	bind off
ITR	in-the-round
m1	'make 1' increase by knitting first into the back loop of a stitch and then into the front loop of the same stitch
t1	'take 1' increase by pulling up a loop from under the crossbar connecting two consecutive stitches
r	rows
rnd(s)	round(s)

Why Knit from the Top Down?

Knitting a sweater from the top down is a logical progression: yoke follows neckline, hem follows body, and finally the sleeves and cuffs. After the neckline stitches are cast on, there's only one direction to go, and that's down to the hem.

Seams are eliminated, which leads to a better fit and more finished appearance. There's little to sew together (usually just the underarm holes), and there are no unsightly seam lines running up and down the sides of your garment.

Top-down knitting also allows for easier fitting and shaping. Because a top-down garment is made in one piece from the start, you can try it on at various stages to get the best fit possible, making adjustments along the way. Need your sleeves longer? Just keep knitting. Need them shorter? Just rip out and bind off. It's fun to see the garment evolve as you make it.

And finally, top-down knitting makes it easy to incorporate ornamentation and other details, such as stitch texture, beading, and shaping, into your design. By reducing or even eliminating fit and sizing issues, you can focus on the styling—the twists and turns of a ruffled cuff, or tapering the body to add a little zing.

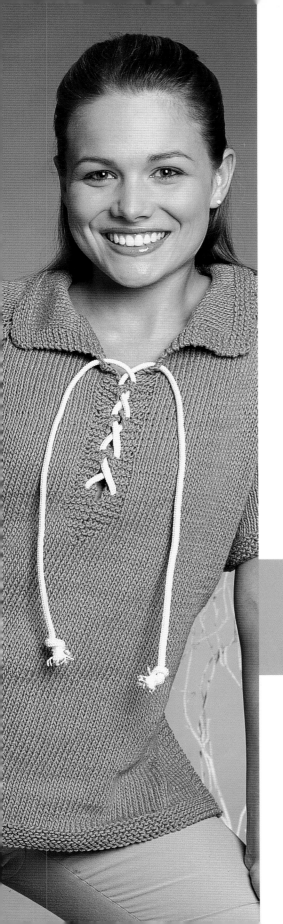

The biggest difference between top-down construction and traditional piecemeal knitting is that the former is worked in one piece, whereas piecemeal sweaters are by definition completed piece by piece. Pullovers made using the top-down method are worked entirely in the round (ITR). For cardigans, the sleeves are worked (ITR) and the body is worked back and forth (B&F). Sound confusing? Read on.

Your knitting equipment will be different, too. To achieve the seamless perfection of a top-down sweater, circular needles (cn) and double-pointed needles (dpn) are the tools of the trade. Lastly, traditional (B&F) knitting is worked in rows (r), whereas top-down (ITR) knitting is worked in rounds (rnds).

Knitting (ITR) requires an ability to work with cn and dpn needles. You will also need to learn how to achieve the same stitch pattern while going from one method to the other. For example, to create a garter stitch working (B&F), you just knit every row, whereas when working (ITR), the same effect is achieved by alternating knit and purl rounds. Here are some of the more common similarities and differences:

STITCH PATTERN   HOW TO ACHIEVE BASIC STITCH PATTERN

	(B & F)	Top-Down (ITR)
Garter stitch	k all rows	k 1 rnd, p 1 rnd, repeat 2 rnds
Stockinette stitch	k 1 row. p 1 row—repeat those 2 rows	k all rnds

Reading and Understanding Top-Down Patterns

Before you begin to cast on to make a top-down sweater, take a moment to read through these general pattern outlines—one for pullovers, one for cardigans. They will give you an overall idea of how a top-down sweater is formed. Pay particular attention to the round or row where you will be placing markers to denote the yoke increases. The proper placement of these markers is the key to forming the sleeve and body parts correctly. They'll eventually indicate where you divide the yoke once it's finished. For novices, I recommend starting with the simplest form: a pullover with a straight body (no shaping), long, tapered sleeves, and the neck design of your choice.

Basic Pullover Pattern

collar (work ITR)
Start with a 16"/40cm circular needle (cn). Stitches are cast on starting at the outermost edge of the collar or neckline. Without twisting the cast-on stitches, connect the two sides and work as instructed.

yoke (work ITR)
To form the yoke, place markers (pm) at designated positions around the collar. These markers indicate where increases will be made to expand your yoke down and outward, creating the front and back of the sweater and the shoulders (which eventually form the sleeves). This first round is called the "set-up round." Set-up rounds (rnds) commonly read as follows:

Rnd 1: k____sts (front sts), pm,
k____sts (sleeve sts), pm,
k____sts (back sts), pm,
k____sts (sleeve sts), pm.

Recount your stitches and check marker placement.

The next row is the first increase row, where eight (8) sts will be added—2 on either side of each marker. Markers must be slipped (sl m) from one needle to the other as you work to note where increases have to be made as the yoke is worked around.

Rnd 2 (Inc rnd):
m1, *k to 1 st before marker, m1, sl m, m1, repeat from ** around for each marker, end m1.

Rnd 3: Work across without any increases.

The yoke is formed by repeating Rnds 2 and 3 for as many times as the pattern specifies, until it reaches the underarm. Try on the sweater to make sure the yoke is long enough. While knitting the yoke, you'll need to switch to the longer cn's to accommodate the growing number of stitches.

Increases on either side of the markers can be accomplished in a number of ways, depending on how you want the garment to look. To help you decide which increase technique to use, refer to page 25.

body (work ITR)
Divide up the stitches on various cn and/or stitch holders so the body can be worked separately from the two sleeves. You'll need several extra cn's for holding the sleeve stitches while you work the body stitches. A typical yoke division round reads as follows:

Using the main cn:
k____(front) sts, CO 1 st (underarm ease—the number of stitches varies by pattern), pm (to denote body side), CO 1 st (underarm ease), Slip ____(~~left~~ right sleeve) sts on a 16"/40cm cn to be worked later, *(or slip onto a length of yarn)*
k_____ (back) sts,
CO 1 st (underarm ease), pm (to denote body side), CO 1 st (underarm ease) place ____(~~right~~ left sleeve) sts on 16"/40cm cn to be worked later.

The front and the back stitches should now be on the main cn needle along with the stitches and markers that you have added at the underarms. The explanations in the parentheses above are added only for your benefit—most patterns don't include them.

Tips for Top-Down Success

DON'T GET STUCK IN CONVENTION. For example, in the past, patterns usually specified two needle sizes: one for the cuffs and collar, and one for the body of the sweater. But today, the options for style and detail have opened up. Experiment to achieve the look and result you desire. Make swatches before you start a knitting project. Save your swatches, keep a record of what you do, and learn from your own knitting experience.

KNITTING IS NOT A SCIENCE. You have to know the basics—how to cast on, bind off, or make a simple knit or purl stitch, for starters. But after that, designing a garment is up to you. You decide the pattern and style you want. Knitted fabric always has stretch and give to it, so you don't need the same degree of precision in shape-making as required for sewing. You might want to knit a smaller, shorter, or narrower shape to hug your form. Which leads to the next point...

KNITTING IS VERY MUCH AN ART. Technique has to be mastered and there is always more than one way to do things. Experiment to understand how different fibers work, how a yarn works up with various needle sizes, and how combining fibers affects the outcome. There's also color and texture; experiment as if you were an artist mixing paints on a palette.

MATH COUNTS. There's much to be learned about geometry and algebra in a sweater. At the very least, you must understand the concept of gauge—the number of stitches per inch for a given set of yarn and needles. This concept alone will take you far as a hand knitter.

AND FINALLY, there's always an alternative way of doing things: casting on, decreasing, increasing, binding off, etc. Experiment to determine the best way to get where you want to go. Take "should" out of your vocabulary and look at designing as problem— solving rather than rule-following.

Now, work the body of the sweater (ITR). Try the sweater on before you join the front and back to make sure the fit is correct. Use several cns, so that you can stretch the garment over your head without dropping stitches.

The sweater body can be worked straight without further shaping. If you want to shape the body for a more form-fitting structure, you can decrease stitches along the side seams or create darts down the front and back (see page 27).

hem (work ITR)
After you've knitted the body to the desired length, follow the pattern instructions to complete the hem or alter the design (see page 28). Try the sweater on once again to check length before you bind off (BO) loosely.

sleeves (work ITR)
Each sleeve will be worked separately on either 16"/40cm cn or double-pointed needles (dpn). If you don't have enough stitches to make it comfortably around a cn, then use dpn (you should be able to use cn for at least 1"/2.5cm or so before switching to dpns). Most often you will end up using dpns anyway, as the number of stitches quickly diminishes when you make the underarm decreases required for a tapered sleeve. Sleeve instructions typically read as follows:

Using 16"/40cm cn, CO 1 st, pm, CO 1 st (at the underarm, for ease, but the number varies by pattern).

Slip marker as you work around: k for 1"/2.5cm, ending at underarm.

For a straight sleeve, with no shaping: work ITR to desired length.

For a tapered sleeve: dec at the underarm on either side of the marker, as follows (remembering to shift to dpn as sleeve sts diminish):

K2tog, k around, k2tog.

Repeat last rnd, every 4th rnd, ____ times.

Patterns will always indicate the intervals of dec rnds and how many you'll have to complete. If you are designing your own sweater, you'll have to do a bit of math (see page 34).

cuff (work ITR)
Try on your sweater to check the length, then follow the pattern directions for the cuff. BO loosely.

finishing
Sew together seams under the arm and weave in ends.

Basic Cardigan Pattern

Unlike a pullover, in which both the body and the sleeves are worked ITR, only the sleeves of the cardigan are done this way. The cardigan yoke and body are worked B&F, but still on a cn (to accommodate the large number of sts). When knitting ITR, you are always working with the right side (RS) facing. However, with cardigans, you're turning the work from one side to the other, so you'll need to know which is the right side (RS) and which is the wrong side (WS).

collar (work B&F)
Start at the outer edge and work toward the neckline. Cast on the specified number of stitches and work the collar B&F. You can work on straight needles until the number of stitches makes doing so unwieldy.

yoke (work B&F)
Divide up the stitches and place markers to begin the yoke increases. You'll need at least four (4) markers to delineate the sleeves and body front and back. It's also helpful (but optional) to add two more markers to denote the beginning and end of the front band stitches. A typical set-up row reads as follows:

Row 1 (RS):—Set-up rnd and place markers

k_____ (front left band) sts, pm,
k ____ (left front) sts, pm,
k ____ (sleeve) sts, pm,
k ____ (back) sts, pm,
k ____ (sleeve) sts, pm,
k____ (right front) sts, pm,
k____(right front band) sts.

Row 2 and all even rows (WS): sl 1, p across.

Note: Alternating k and p rows will produce a stockinette st, so if you want the front bands to be in garter st, the first and last 2 to 5 sts (depending on how wide you want the band) will always be knit sts. To achieve a smooth outer edge, slip the first stitch in each row.

The third row is the first inc row where 8 sts will be added, 2 on either side of the 4 inside markers (not the ones denoting the front bands).

Row 3 (RS): sl 1, k_____ (left front _within 1 st of_ band) sts, sl m, *k to next marker, m1, sl m, m1, repeat from * across for next three markers, work across to last marker, sl m, k ____ (right front band) sts.

Repeat Rows 2 and 3 the number of times designated in the pattern. End by finishing a row 2.

body (work B&F)

Using the main cn, regroup the stitches to create the body and sleeves as follows:

Row 1 (RS): divide the yoke sts into front, back, and two sleeves, sl 1, k

____ (left front band) sts, sl m,
k____ (left front) sts, CO 1 st, pm (underarm), CO 1 st,
place sleeve sts on cn holder,
k ____ (back) sts, CO 1 st, pm (underarm), CO 1 st,
place sleeve sts on holder,
k____ (right front) sts, sl m,
k____ (right front band) sts.

Note: The number of sts CO at the underarm will varies by pattern.

Row 2: sl 1, p across (working the two front bands in garter st if specified).

Repeat Rows 1 and 2 for the desired length.

The sweater body can be worked straight without further shaping. For a more form-fitting structure, you can dec sts along the side seams or create darts down the front and back (see page 27).

hem (work ITR)

Follow the pattern instructions to complete the hem or alter it to your taste (see page 28). Try on the sweater to check length before you bind off (BO) loosely.

sleeves (work ITR)

Cardigan sleeves are worked in the same way as pullover sleeves (see page 14).

Understanding Sizing and Size Charts

Sizing is an elusive concept, at least in the United States, where there is no national standard measurement for body shapes. The good news is that some trade organizations have taken the lead in establishing standards for their particular industries. Most yarn manufacturers and knitting designers follow the standards set by the Craft Yarn Council of America (www.craftyarncouncil.com). Those guidelines were used for this collection.

The easiest way to determine which size you want to make is to refer to the *actual finished garment measurement*. This is especially important, as people have different preferences for how they want to wear a garment. Some like tight-fitting garments, whereas others want a looser fit. The Craft Yarn Council has also considered this and has defined fit terminology as follows:

TYPE OF FIT	DESCRIPTION
Very close fitting	Actual chest/bust measurement or less
Close fitting	1–2"/2.5–5cm
Standard fitting	2–4"/5–10cm
Loose fitting	4–6"/10–15cm
Oversized	6"/15cm or more

Again, the safest bet is to look at the *actual measurement* of the completed *garment*.

In this book, size and gauge options also differ from past writings on one-piece knitting. Top-down patterns used to offer myriad sizes based on chest size, measured in 1"/2.5cm increments. Here, we've distilled this approach and use only four basic sizes—S, M, L, XL—again, based on the Craft Yarn Council's standards.

On the other hand, gauge options have been expanded dramatically. Top-down patterns used to be written mainly for tried-'n'-true worsted yarn. Nowadays, however, there are many yarn options in the market, so there's a real need to have patterns that will accommodate the many choices available.

The really good news is that the basic patterns in this book (pages 114 to 125) are expressed in *eight gauges* for both standard pullover and cardigan shapes. These patterns provide outlines to help you get started in designing your own styles. Once you get the hang of knitting top-down sweaters, you can begin to tailor the patterns further and hone them to your personal measurements. Refer to the Top-Down Math section (page 34) to assist you in making any alterations.

The charts at right will also be a useful reference point when making further alterations. For example, you might observe that the average long-arm length for a Medium is 17"/43cm. But if you know that your arms are longer or shorter, you can make a note of that and add or subtract a ball or two to your final yarn purchase.

SWEATER SIZING (INCHES)

Sizes	S	M	L	XL
Chest				
actual chest size	32 –34	36 – 38	40 – 42	44- 46
finished garment *	36	40	44	48
Neckline				
slightly dropped, front starts at base of neck hole	16	17	18	19
Yoke				
top of mid-shoulder to underarm	8 1/2-9	9 1/2 -10	10 -11	11 –11 1/2
Body				
short: underarm to below bust	4	5	6	6 1/2
mid-length: underarm to hip	11	12	13	13 1/2
long: underarm to below hip	14	15	16	16 1/2
Sleeve				
short: underarm to mid-bicep	4	4 1/2	5	5 1/2
three-quarter sleeve: underarm to lower elbow	9	10	11	11 1/2
long: underarm to wrist	17	17 1/2	18	18 1/2
cuff circumference	8	9	10	10

* See page 21 [handwritten "21" over "24"] for a discussion of neckline sizing

SWEATER SIZING (CM)

Sizes	S	M	L	XL
Chest				
actual chest size	81-86	92-97	102-107	112-117
finished garment	91	102	112	123
Neckline				
slightly dropped, front starts at base of neck hole	41	43	46	48
Yoke				
top of mid-shoulder to underarm	22-23	24-25	25-27	27-28
Body				
short: underarm to below bust	10	13	15	16.5
mid-length: underarm to hip	28	30.5	33	34
long: underarm to below hip	35.5	38	41	42
Sleeve				
short: underarm to mid-bicep	10	11	13	14
three-quarter sleeve: underarm to lower elbow	23	25	28	29
long: underarm to wrist	43	44	46	47
cuff circumference	20	23	25	25

* See page 21 for a discussion of neckline sizing

Designing a Sweater

Designing a sweater or any other garment is a matter of making a series of decisions that eventually add up to a complete look or style. Visualizing what you want is key, so making a sketch is always helpful. It doesn't have to be a perfect drawing, just something to help you edit your thoughts and ideas. Ask yourself the following questions as a way to think about developing your design:

Function

How will you wear the sweater? Will it be worn:

- as casual or formal wear?

- during the day or evening or both?

- as outerwear, requiring a heavy-gauge yarn; or indoors or as a layering piece, which calls for a lighter weight yarn?

- to complement or coordinate with other wardrobe elements?

Form

What basic shape or style do you want to make—pullover or cardigan? Some people prefer one shape over the other, but you may also want to consider when and where you will wear the garment:

Cardigans have open fronts with or without buttons or some other closure, which allows you to:

- take the sweater easily off and on—an advantage especially for the elderly or disabled, or even for those concerned with messing up a hairstyle.

- easily layer another piece underneath.

Front cardigan closures (such as buttons and zippers) are often necessary, but for a cleaner, more minimal look, you may want to eliminate them and just knit front bands down the two front sides of the cardigan.

Pullovers, usually, but not always, seem more casual. They also can:

- appear neater than cardigans, because there are no open flaps to flop open.

- keep out chest chill.

Then again, they have to be pulled over the head, which isn't always convenient.

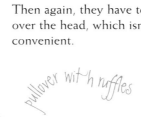
pullover with ruffles

Details and Styling

Details make or break a garment. Perhaps the most important factors to consider are shape and length of both arms and body. For example, if your upper arms aren't your most attractive feature, you might want to avoid a short sleeve, which calls attention to the area. Better yet, you could extend the sleeve to go just over the bicep, stopping just above the crook of the arm—long enough to cover unsightly bulges, yet short enough to still be a short sleeve. One of the most flattering sleeve lengths is the three-quarter-length sleeve. It's a feminine and elegant way to elongate the arm. It also allows you to show off bracelets, see your watch more readily, and do more active things, such as cooking and entertaining, without feeling constrained or accidentally brushing a sleeve through gravy.

Sweater length also hinges on your body proportions. First, you have to figure out what length looks best on you. Narrow-hipped people can wear just about any style. Those with wider hips perhaps have more limited styling options, but not as limited as you may think. For years, stylists suggested buying jackets and sweaters long enough to go over the hips, to "hide" them, but often this only emphasizes the region.

If you don't know what looks good, plan to spend some time in a department store with an honest friend and try on different shapes— things you'd never consider in the past. You may come up with a whole new set of ideas about what looks good on you. Then make a beeline to your favorite yarn store.

Style Tips

With age comes wisdom, or at least a sense of what works and what doesn't work for me. Through time, I've accumulated my own set of style biases, which I'll share with you. Keep in mind that this is my own personal set of rules, but it might help you to think about establishing your own design criteria:

KEEP YOUR COLOR PALETTE SIMPLE
Stick with just a handful of colors (preferably only one or two) for the simple reason that most people tend to look better in solid or simple colors. You won't get tired as quickly of simpler combinations either, which is important, because yarn can be a substantial investment nowadays.

CONSIDER SHAPE JUST AS MUCH AS COLOR
Shape doesn't present itself like color, but keep it in mind as you make your yarn decisions. It's hard to make a dainty ruffle with a bulky-weight yarn, and a fine-gauge yarn won't provide the heft you need for a turtleneck. Shape and color should go hand-in-hand.

CONSIDER INCORPORATING SOME TEXTURE
If you are taking the time to hand knit a sweater, try to do something you don't necessarily see in the stores. Jazz it up a bit with some patterning—however, the simpler the more elegant.

BALANCE DESIGN ELEMENTS
Bold colors make your form stand out, darker colors make it recede. Detail makes the garment and catches the eye, but too much detail can be distracting. Balance color with texture, and don't forget about shape. Less isn't always more—it can be boring. But then again, too much can be downright overwhelming. If in doubt, ask an honest friend.

over time—the heavier you make the piece, the more it will droop. Note, however, that there are always exceptions to the rule: A very fine-gauge silk mohair yarn knit into a puffy-type sleeve number could work well. The great thing about top-down knitting is that you can easily shave away the extra inches from the sweater body and under the arms, and in the process use less wool. So, work to shape your knitting, even if just a bit more than you've done in the past. Stop knitting sweatshirts—you'll avoid looking like a tent and reduce your yarn costs as well!

After you decide on the basic shape and body and sleeve lengths, you'll want to give some thought to further detailing, such as how to finish the cuffs and hem, whether to add texture, how you'll use color, and whether some other non-fiber elements, such as beads or sequins, will be applied. Theoretically, you could pull out the stops and add all sorts of bells and whistles to a design, but it's better to edit yourself. Keep detailing to a minimum; use just enough for added interest. How do you know when too much is too much? This is where a rough sketch comes in handy; it will allow you to see whether the concept is too crowded, too minimal, or just the right balance. It might help to purchase some colored pencils as well, to see the color effects in combination with the detail. And finally, pass your ideas by a friend you respect for his or her personal sense of style. My daughter is my best critic and advisor—I rarely leave the house without her assessment!

While establishing appropriate sleeves and body proportions is crucial, you must also decide whether and how much to shape the body of the sweater. Again, it's a personal preference, hinging most on how you like to wear a garment: some people adore a tight fit; others abhor it. But overall, there's an argument to be made for perhaps tightening up your silhouette, at least a little bit more than the usual knitting pattern shows. Knitted fabric stretches, but too few patterns take advantage of this wonderful property. Fine-gauged knits can look fabulous draped about the body, try not to obscure your figure.

A sweater's silhouette will look better if you minimize excessive fabric by avoiding large billowy sleeves and overly large finished-body widths. Remember also that knitted fabric sags

$\mathcal{E}$lements of a Sweater

In designing a sweater, you'll have to determine the shapes of the various parts—collar, cuffs, sleeves, and body. Here are some ideas to consider.

Necklines and Collars

For the patterns in this book, the collar is the starting point, after which point you immediately begin to establish the yoke. The collar melds into the neckline in one piece—no seams. This means that you'll begin all collars (ruffles included) at their outermost edge and work toward the neckline and the yoke.

The neck circumference, referred to as the *baseline neck* is the most important number in the entire sweater. It's measured from the bottom of the front neck hole. For the size range in this book—S, M, L, XL—the baseline neck circumferences are as follows:

NECK CIRCUMFERENCE

	S	M	L	XL
Baseline neck: falls at bottom of neck hole				
in	16	17	18	19
cm	40.5	42.5	46	48

These figures were used to determine most of the collars and necklines (exceptions are explained further on in the book), and they are the set of figures on which all yoke increases are based. If you want the neckline to start higher (for instance, a turtleneck), it will have to be made tighter.

The following examples briefly describe different collar shapes and what you have to consider in executing them.

ribbed
Ribbing is a classic finish for both ITR and B&F sweaters.

This collar is done ITR in a k2/p2 rib for a pullover.

Extend the collar for a turtleneck...

... which can either be folded over or not.

Ribbing also works well for cardigan collars. in this case the rib is a k1/p1 pattern.

rolled
A rolled collar can also be used for both ITR and B&F designs. The stockinette stitch creates the roll.

Rolled collars can be fashioned to roll inward...

...or outward

ruffled

Ruffled collars look complicated, but are really easy.

For a simple ruffled collar, double the number of stitches needed for the neckline, then work to desired ruffle width and k2tog on the last round. For a more ruffled collar, CO triple or quadruple the stitches required for the neck, and then decrease to neckline on last row.

polo

This collar is classic and easy to make.

CO the number of sts specified by the baseline neckline for your size and yarn gauge, and work the collar to the desired width.

overlapping polo

This collar starts out like the polo, but you have to cast on extra stitches for the overlap.

Start with a simple polo collar, remembering you want to add on extra sts at the beg to overlap.

Once you have kintted the color to the desired width, place the end stitches added for the overlap on a dpn.

Ease the dpn with these sts behind the right side of the wrap-around collar, taking care not to twist the collar.

Knit the first sts from each needle together.

Continue knitting together a stitch from the dpn with its corresponding st on the cn until all the sts on the dpn haves been joined.

Work 2 to 3 rnds to secure the overlap. Place yoke markers in the last round.

mandarin

A mandarin collar can be made as high as you like and looks best fitted close to the neck. You need to knit twice the height of the collar desired because you will fold it over (a ridge is knitted to do so).

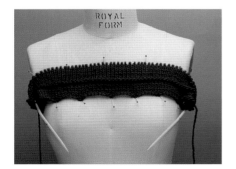

CO the required number of neckline sts and work St st to the height desired; then p 2 rows for a ridge row and resume the St st again to match the front section width.

Fold over the collar and sew the ends together.

After you have worked some of the yoke, tack down the collar on the ws with an overhand stitch.

hood

A hood is made the exact same way as the polo collar (work straight up from the neckline). The only difference is that it's longer and then it's seamed at the top.

Front view

Sew up the seam at the top of the hood.

Back view

Side view

tube for drawstring or ribbon

A tube is formed like the mandarin collar, but without the purl ridge row. Just CO the number of stitches required for the baseline neck and knit a width that, when folded, creates the tube.

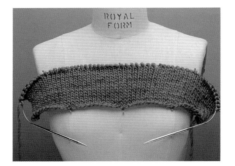

This is what the tube looks like unfolded.

Once the yoke has been worked a bit, fold it towards the neck and tack down.

cowl

A cowl is an oversized, droopy turtleneck formed by doubling or tripling the number of stitches on the outer edge of the collar before it's decreased to meet the number of baseline neck sts. The finer the gauge, yarn the droopier the effect.

In a bulkier yarn, a cowl has a more subtle drape.

Fine-gauge yarn creates a droopy effect.

The Yoke

The four points of increase on the yoke—two down the front and two down the back—form the two sleeves and back and front body parts. Increases are made on either side of each marker, and these increase rnds or rows are done alternately with a non-increase or plainly worked rnd or row. Increases appear differently depending on the increase method used.

M1 is an increase stitch in which you 'make-a-stitch' by knitting in the back loop and then in the front loop of a stitch. It makes a tight-seam look. No holes should be created.

Knit in back loop.

Knit in front loop.

A T1 increase creates a lacy effect. It's an increase stitch made by taking a stitch between 2 sts from the row below.

A completed 'T1.'

An M1 increase creates a tighter seam than a T1 increase.

Hints and Collected Wisdom

Casting on. For a loose, but even edge when casting on, use two needles of the same size held together. When you're finished, pull out the needle you won't be using.

Easing stitches. To ensure that you don't pull your work too tightly when making bobbles or doing two-color work, stick your finger or fingertip behind the work and pull the color in use over your finger. When you switch to the next color, repeat placing your finger or fingertip underneath the strand on the backside of the work.

Knit to fit. Try the sweater on as you knit. Make sure the drop from the shoulder to the underarm is long enough. You can extend the yoke by knitting a few more rounds after the increase rounds. Check the arm length. Check the length of the garment to the hem as well as the width around the hip or waist. If you want the garment to be tighter after the yoke is completed, make decreases along the sides. If you need a wider girth, do the reverse.

design elements for the yoke
The yoke itself can embody a variety of design elements. Texture, such as raised lines in "Ember" (below), is a nice addition.

Beads and sequins can add interest as well. Stringed sequins were used for "Stardust"(page 105), and wooden beads for "Breeze" (page 99).

The yoke shape can also be altered, as in the split fronts of "Coast" (page 96) and "Cherry Blossom" (page 81).

Body Shape

After the yoke has been formed, the stitches on the cable needle must be separated and allocated so that you can work the body apart from the sleeves. It's always handy to have a few extra cable needles around to hold the sleeve stitches while working the body. By the time you finish the yoke, you will have added enough stitches on your needle so that the circumference of the body (the front and back stitches) is equal to the chest measurement for your size. Now you have to decide whether you are going to work the body straight to the hem or lower edge or whether you'd like to shape it. Working the body straight is easy—just knit. Shaping takes a bit more thought, but it's not hard at all with the top-down technique. Shaping involves decreasing sts—using k2togs—at regular and strategic points down the length of the sweater body.

shaping down the sides

The easiest way to shape the body is to take incremental decreases down the sides of the body, which means that when you are dividing up the yoke sts into the various sweater parts, be sure to place two markers at the underarms on the body sts. Those markers will indicate where to decrease. Now you have to decide on your fit. Use your established chest measurement as the starting point. If you have made a 40"/102cm chest, for example, but would like to whittle the sweater away to show off your 36"/92cm waist, you'll need to decrease 4"/10cm from the underarm to the waist, 2"/5cm on either side (see figure 1). Use the gauge to calculate the 4"/10cm decrease into the number of

sts you need to eliminate (4 x gauge). Don't forget that you are going to work these decreases on either side of the two markers that were placed under the arms (see figure 2). As you can see, it's just simple math.

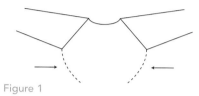

Figure 1

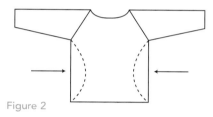

Figure 2

Shaping can also be done in the form of darts—two in the front and two in the back—much the same way as a shirt is shaped (see figure 3). Again, do the math and then place markers where the darts should begin.

Figure 3

Other ways to trim a silhouette are by using ribbing at the sides, as in "Violet" (right), or by inserting eyelets to string belts and ribbons to take in the waist, as in "Wild Plum" (above right).

The Lower Edge or Hem

The hem or lower edge of the body is the final detail. A tried-and-true way to get the hem to lay flat is to create ribbing. Garter stitch, seed stitch, or moss stitch also help push the fabric flat. You can also use a heavier yarn for the hem or even add beads, the weight of which may also hold down the edge. Fringe and ruffles work, too, and by all means experiment. After the practical consideration of form, design elements such as lace borders and peplums are easily achieved with top-down techniques as well. Peplums work best if the body has been taken in at the waist (see page 27 for side shaping), then you double or even triple the sts in the waist rnd or row and work downward. Some of the edgings used in the book are:

ribbed
Ribbing is the traditional way to finish a sweater. Make sure you are working with an even multiple of sts. For example, a k1/p1 rib has a multiple of 2, so you'll need a st count divisible by 2. If you happen to have an extra st, just k2tog at the beg of the first rnd, and then establish your rib pattern. A k2/p2 rib is a multiple of 4, a k3/p3 is a multiple of 6, etc.

garter and seed
Garter stitch and seed stitch neatly flatten a knitted fabric and are subtle and all-purpose enough to use with other design elements.

ridged and tubed
Other textured stitches, especially those that run horizontally, also establish a neat lower edge.

Also try ruffles, fringes, or even irregularly shaped edges. Slant the front hem one way and the back the other, or mirror slants on both the front and the back so that the lower edge comes to a point off to one side.

Sleeves

By the time you're ready to do the sleeves, the body has already been finished (the shape of which might dictate how to shape the sleeves). The easiest sleeve to make is to work straight without shaping. If you want to taper the sleeve, see page 37 for instructions on how to work out the number of sts to taper. In addition to the shaping, you'll want to decide on a sleeve length. Here are some ideas and shapes to consider:

Cap sleeves, as in "Cherry Blossom" (see page 81), are made by working no more than 1"/2.5cm beyond the yoke and then binding off.

Short sleeves can range from 2"/5cm to 6"/12cm beyond the yoke. You might also want to create a cuff, so you'll need to knit a few extra inches to be able to turn it upward. For emphasis, use another color or texture for the upturned part.

My all-time favorite is the three-quarter-length sleeve, because it flatters most body types.

Long sleeves emphasize the elegance of the entire arm and keep you warm. Another way to make a long sleeve is to extend the cuff up the arm.

cuffs

Remember that sleeve length includes the cuff. Also make sure your cuff design works with the body hem. Here are some ideas to consider:

ribbed

This is the real workhorse of sleeve ends, but again, check that your stitch multiple is an even number when making a rib pattern.

folded up

Knit a few extra inches at the bottom of the sleeve—enough to fold the cuff up. Tack it down with a running stitch and/or place a button for an accent. Coordinate the button design with buttons used on the front of a cardigan.

rolled

This is really more of an edge than a cuff. If you knit a St st sleeve straight and end off, the lower edge will roll upward. You can also invert the edge to make it roll inward by purling ITR. It's a good way to deal with novelty trims at edges, because ribbing constricts the look of some of the fluffier trims.

scarf tie

Think of tying off the end of a sleeve with leather, lacing, or even with a scarf tie knitted right from the sleeve itself. To do so, after you have worked the sleeve length, add the amount of sts you need to get the length of tie you desire (at least 5"/12cm worth of sts) on either end of the needle. Work these sts back and forth to the desired width (make the tie just wide enough so that you can knot it once it's finished. Try using a contrasting color, yarn, or texture for the knitted tie.

ruffled

Ruffles are a joyous way to end a sleeve and are easy to achieve. When you've worked the sleeve to the desired length, increase in every st on the last rnd, then keep working until you arrive at the ruffle width you desire. If you want an even fluffier ruffle, work the first inc rnd, then work a plain rnd, and then work another inc rnd, increasing in only every second or third st around. Try making the ruffle a different color or pattern than the body of the sweater—think lace.

ornamentation

Just about any sort of ornamentation can be knitted in or applied to a lower sleeve edge. You can work in a design such as bobbles or apply beads and sequins.

As with the hem, other ideas to consider for the lower edges of sleeves include fringe, picot, lace, a fabric cuff (split the edge, fold it back, and sew), or even a crochet cuff.

Cardigan Closures

You'll have to decide whether you want the front of your cardigan to have some type of closure or not. If you don't use a closure, you'll have to decide how you are going to work the two front edges of the cardigan so that they look finished when complete. You can work the edges plain in St st, but most likely you'll want to have some type of border or edge that remains flat. Garter, seed, and moss patterns work well, but also consider cabled panels or some other decorative stitch encased in an increase panel.

Closures for cardigan fronts can run the gamut from a simple button at the top to multiple buttons down the front. How much do you want the cardigan to close—partially or completely? Several buttons grouped along the bands can be interesting. Here are other ideas to consider:

partial front closure
Leather ties cut from lightweight cowhide were used to secure the top and middle of this cardigan.

top-only devices
All sorts of devises can be used for top closures: one or two oversized buttons; one small one, ties or lacings; a frog; or even a brooch or pin.

total-front closure
Buttons are perhaps most commonly used to for cardigan closures, but also consider zippers, snaps, and other toggle mechanisms.

**combination top closure
and several buttons**
If you can't decide on just one method to close your sweater, incorporate two, as with the Peony sweater above. The top is secured with a scarf tie, but just below it is an almost invisible but charming row of three shell buttons aligned one after the other at the top.

ornamentation

As you can see, lots of details and decisions go into sweater design. Usually, I think about shape first, then color, and finally ornamentation. But a trim, bead, or novelty yarn can also become the departure point. Play around with ideas and materials in your head and on paper—sometimes the strangest juxtapositions lead to eureka moments!

Because they are positioned on the outermost parts of the sweater, collars and cuffs are often focal points. The shape of the collar and cuffs can set the tone for the sweater, but the yarn type and color also play a part. You can visually blend the cuffs and collar into the sweater body and yoke by using the same yarn throughout, or you can accentuate them by working them in contrasting yarns or texture. This is precisely the spot for that gorgeous ball of novelty yarn you've been coveting!

Top-Down Math

You can easily use this book without ever having to delve into the behind-the-scenes math; just follow the patterns as you would any other. However, understanding the why and wherefore of the numbers will enable you to alter the basic patterns and ultimately help you to expand your own design options.

NECK CIRCUMFERENCE

	S	M	L	XL
Baseline neck: falls at bottom of neck hole				
in	16	17	18	19
cm	40.5	42.5	46	48
Tighter neck: hits top of neck hole				
in	15	16	17	17.5
cm	38	40.5	43	44.5
Tightest neck: neck circumference				
In	14.5	15	15.5	16
cm	37	38	39	40.5

Calculating Cast-On Stitches at the Neckline

The most important number in a top-down sweater pattern is the stitch count for the neckline—the baseline neck. This produces a garment with a neck circumference that will touch the bottom of the neck hole for that given size. If you want a tighter neckline, use the neck circumference chart below, left. Make the collar with fewer stitches (as dictated by a narrower neck), but when you get ready to start the yoke, add enough stitches in the last row of the collar equal to the baseline neck number for the garment size and yarn gauge you are using.

To determine the number of stitches needed for the baseline neck, multiply the baseline neck circumference by the yarn gauge:

Cast-On Stitches (CO)
=Baseline neck circumference (in or cm)
x yarn gauge (sts/in or cm)

So for example, to make a Large sweater in a 5-gauge yarn (sts/in or cm), you will need to cast on 90 sts: 18 in x 5 st/in.

The baseline neck number also helps determine how to construct the collar. For the example, you'll cast on 90 sts to make a polo collar, simple round neck, etc. However, for a simple ruffle collar, you'll have to double the CO sts because you're beginning the ruffle at its outermost edge (the fluffy side). You'll cast on at least 180 sts (90 x 2). After you have worked the desired ruffle width, k2tog across arrive at the desired number of baseline neck sts, ready to begin the yoke.

Let's do a calculation for a tighter collar or neckline. For example, to make a turtleneck with a chunky yarn (3 sts/in) in size Small, refer to the chart (below, left) which says that you'll require a neck circumference of 14.5"/37cm. Multiply this number by the gauge of the chunky yarn (3 sts/in) to get to the number of sts that you have to cast on to work the collar. You'll come out with 43.5, but round up to get 44 sts.

14.5"/37cm x 3 sts/in gauge
= 43.5, round up to 44

Work the turtleneck ITR for 6 to 7"/15 to 18cm, depending on your neck length. When it's complete, work 1 row plain, increasing to the number of sts to reach the baseline number for your size sweater and yarn gauge. So you'll need to increase the number of your stitches to reach a 16"/40.5cm neckline at a gauge of 3 sts/in:

16"/40.5cm x 3 sts/in gauge = 48

Which means, you'll have to add only 4 sts on the last row to reach the baseline (48 sts - 44 sts = 4 sts).

Again, remember that before you start the increase of the yoke, you have to return to the number of baseline sts required for your size and weight of yarn.

Establishing the Yoke

Many top-down patterns describe how to "short-row" the back section before starting the yoke increases, allowing the front to lay forward, which, the argument goes, makes for a better fitting sweater. However, if not done absolutely properly, this technique can leave holes at the turns.

Here's an easier method that works just as well. It's based on how the CO sts are divided up to create the front, back, and sleeves. In sum, allocate more stitches to the front section than to the back, so that the sweater will in effect be "front-heavy." This creates the same effect as short-rowing and provides greater room on the front of the sweater, where most women are larger.

Using the example of 90 sts (required for a large sweater in yarn gauge 5 st/in or cm), divide by 3 to get 30: one-third sts for the front, one-third for the back, and one-third for the sleeves. If you get fractions, round down for the sleeves, or round up for the back and front, but check to make sure that after rounding you still have the same total you began with (in this case, 90 sts):

Front	30
Back	30
Sleeve	30/2 =15
Sleeve	30/2 =15
TOTAL	90

Next, readjust the sleeve allocations so that the number of sts for each sleeve equals only 2"/5cm worth along the neckline. For this example, that means allocating 12 sts for each sleeve (2" x 5 sts/in or cm (yarn gauge). Add the leftover sleeve stitches (15 st − 10 sts) = 5 sts per sleeve, or 2 x 5 = 10 sts, to the front stitch allocation for a total of 40 sts. Your stitches will be "front-loaded."

Front	30
Back	30
Sleeve	30/2 =10
Sleeve	30/2 =10
TOTAL	90

For the basic patterns on pages 114 to 125, I used a slightly different allocation method, with hardly a difference except for a stitch here and there. The results are essentially the same—the front gets a disproportionate amount of stitches.

Calculating the Number of Increase Rows in the Yoke

After you've established your baseline neck sts and divvied them up on the cn using markers, you'll start to work the yoke. This is done by alternating an increase rnd with a non-increase row. An increase rnd is one in which you increase one stitch on either side of each of the four markers that separate the front, back, and sleeve sts. After you have completed one inc round, you'll have added 8 sts (2 sts for every marker). After an increase rnd, work one row without increases. Alternating these two rows forms the yoke. So how many times do you repeat them?

Determining the number of increase rows starts with the chest measurement. For the large size, the chest measurement is 44"/112cm. Multiply this measurement by your gauge, in this case, 5 sts/in:

Chest circumference (finished garment)
x gauge (sts/in or cm)
= number of sts for chest measurement

You get 220 sts, which represents the total number of sts on the cn, the front, back and CO sts at the underarm that you want to arrive at once the yoke increases have been made.

To calculate the number of increase rnds needed, take the difference between the chest measurement in sts and the neckline measurement and divide by 4 (not 8), because 4 is the number of sts added to the body section—front and back—in each increase rnd.

Garment chest measurement
(expressed in sts)
– (baseline neck + front sts) /4
= number of increase rows in the neck

Using the example, you'll get the following:

220 total sts for 44" chest/gauge of 5 sts/in
(40 starting front sts + 30 starting backsts)/4
= 37.5 increase rnds

In this example, we get 37.5 inc rnds, which means that we need 75 total rnds (37.5 x 2), alternating an increase rnd with a non-inc rnd, to make the yoke. However (and this is where the art of knitting comes in), at a vertical gauge of 7 rnds per inch (remember each yarn has a row gauge as well), the armhole that extends longer than desired. So, at this point, I make an artistic decision to keep the most increase rows I can to get to my chest measurement while avoiding creating an extended armhole. I do this by lopping of 2 inc rows. After I finish 35 increase rows, I stop, then I add 4 sts on the body at the underarm to get as close to the 220 chest sts desired. In the end, I get a total of 218 sts, which is close enough to the 220 sts needed for a 44"/112cm chest.

Shaping the Body

The basic idea behind shaping is to calculate the difference in body width from start to finish and express this measurement in stitches. In doing so, remember to work with finished garment measurements.

Let's take the example of tapering to the waist versus just knitting a straight body shape. Begin with the garment chest measurement (which is determined by the number of sts on the main cn needle after the yoke has been worked, after the sleeve sts have been held aside, and after any sts have been added at the underarm on the body sides). In our example, we have 218 sts at this point. Let's decide to take the waist in by 3"/7.6cm, which means that 15 sts (3"/7.6cm x 5 sts/in gauge) need to be decreased. This can be done a number of ways, depending on how you want it to look. If you knit down to the waist and then decrease the entire 15 sts in one rnd, the garment will take on a blouson look. A more tapered look is achieved by making two darts down the front and two down the back, and dividing the 15 sts among these four points. But by far the easiest thing to do is to take regular, incremental decreases down the sides of the body, tapering to the waist. Because we also want to make an even number of decreases (2 sts on either side of the side markers), we'll round our number up to get an even number, making 15 sts into 16 sts for the sake of ease.

Now you'll have to determine how to space the 16-st dec along the side body. First, work the body about 1"/2.5cm straight before you begin your decreases to prevent any bunching under the arms. Remember to place two markers, one at each underarm to designate the decrease locations. Divide the number of stitches you want to eliminate by the number of decrease locations (in this case, by 2 for each side) for an 8-st dec per side. Then decide how you want to decrease—by 1 st on each side for a very gradual taper or by 2 sts on each side for a more dramatic one. Next, measure from your underarm to your waist (your result should be in the range of 6 to 8"/15 to 18cm) and subtract 2"/5cm because the armhole hangs lower. You can also try on the yoke and measure the distance from its lower edge to your waist. Then, multiply that measurement by the rnds/in of your yarn (this should tell you how many rnds you need to work to reach your waist, which will indicate how to divide up the increases along the sides). Remember to deduct the 1"/2.5cm that you worked on the body from the yoke to start. For our example, you'd need to work 6"/15cm to get from the bottom of the yoke to the waist, minus 1"/2.5cm already worked, for 5"/13cm. This means we'll have to work 35 rnds (5 x 7 rnds/in for the yarn in the example) (see box above, right for rnd/row gauges). So you'll want to decrease 8 sts each side within these 35 rnds. Since 16 sts need to be decreased, you'll need to work 4 dec rnd where one st gets eliminated either side of the 2 dec markers. To determine the interval, at which a dec rnd occurs, divide the rounds that must be worked from the base of the yoke to the waist (35 rnds) by the number of dec rnds (4) needed. That comes out to 8.75 (round up to 9). Now you know that once a dec rnd is worked, you'll have to complete 8 rnds before completing another dec rnd.

First, check the yarn label. The row or rnd per inch should be listed there. However, don't rely on that number alone. Always make a swatch of your yarn and measure. The chart below offers approximations, as a guideline.

Approximate Rounds or Rows by Gauge

Yarn type	Sts/in or 2.5 cm	Rnds/row/in or 2.5 cm
Bulky	2	2-2.5
	2.5	3-3.5
Chunky	3	4-4.5
	3.5	4-5
Heavy Worsted	4	5-5.5
	4.5	5-6
DK Worsted	5	6-7
	5.5	7

Calculating Tapered Sleeve Decreases

This is the same principle as described for body shaping —calculate the difference in sts between your starting and end points to determine the number of sts you need to decrease.

It might help to visualize the process, so have a piece of paper and a pencil at hand to sketch out what you are doing. Start by outlining a sleeve and walk through the following calculation, not-

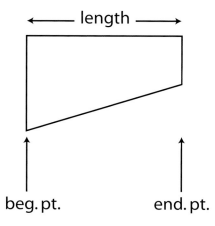

ing the steps on your drawing.

As an example, calculate the taper for a three-quarter-length sleeve by first listing the data you already have. You've finished the yoke, and you know how many sleeve sts you've set aside (80 sts in our example). Divide that number by your yarn gauge—this measures the circumference of your upper arm in inches. For example, the 80 sts divided by 5 sts/in or cm (gauge) gives you 16"/40.5cm. Measure the circumference of your lower arm where you want the sleeve to end. Let's say it's 11"/28cm. Next, measure the length of your arm, starting 1"/2.5cm down from the armpit to a little beyond your elbow—say, 9"/22.5cm.

Data
\# sleeve sts on cn = 80
Circumference, upper arm (in/cm)
= 80 sts/5 sts/in or cm (gauge)
= 16"/40.5cm
Lower arm circumference = 11"/28cm
Length, underarm to sleeve's lower edge
= 11"/28cm

To determine the number of sts you

have to end up with at the lower arm circumference multiply the lower arm circumference by the yarn gauge:

Lower edge sleeve (# sts)
= 11"/28cm circumference
x 5 st/in or cm (gauge)
= 55 sts

Calculate the number of sts to be decreased by taking the number of sts you start with and subtracting the number of sts you want to end up with:

80 sts – 55 sts =
25 sts to be decreased at underarm seam

Because sleeve decreases happen in pairs (one st is dec either side of underarm marker), you'll dec 24 sts (instead of 25) for 12 dec rnds.

24 sts/2 sts per dec per rnd =
12 dec rnds

Now, determine the interval at which these decreases will occur along the length of the sleeve. This is done by determining the number of rows it will take to achieve the 9"/22.5cm length. For our example, we use the full length of the sleeve, minus the initial 1"/2.5cm we worked after the yoke, which equals 8"/20cm (9" - 1" = 8"). Take this 8"/20cm length and multiply it by the row/rnd gauge of your yarn (let's say it's 6 rnds per 1"/2.5cm) to get 48 rnds. This means that the 12 dec rnds (see above) will have to be placed within these 48 rnds. To determine the interval at which the dec rnds will occur, divide the total number of rnds (48) by 12 dec rnds, to get 4. So, for every decrease rnd, you'll work 3 non-dec rnds and make the 5th rnd the dec rnd.

It really is easy—just remember that you're converting length (in/cm) into stitch equivalents to write your knitting directions.

Choosing Yarn and Determining Yardage

Your yarn will dictate what pattern to use or how to write your own (as you know, gauge is all important). Take a look at the basic patterns on page 114 to 125. They are written by gauge, so you'll be able to do just about any top-down sweater using these templates. The following charts will help you to pick out the correct size needles as well.

YARN TYPE, GAUGE, AND NEEDLE SIZE

Wool Weights	Gauge sts per in	sts per 10 cm	Needle Size U.S.	(mm)
Bulky	2–2.5	8–10	11+	8+
Chunky	3–3.5	12–14	9–10	5.5–6
Heavy Worsted	4–4.5	16–18	7–8	4.5–5
DK Weight	5–5.5	20–22	6–7	4–4.5

American	1	2	3	4	5	6	7	8	9	10	10.5	11	13	15
Metric (mm)	2.5	2.75	3.25	3.5	3.75	4	4.5	5	5.5	6	6.5	8	9	10

Note: After you've determined your needle size, make a sample swatch. Don't depend on the yarn label for the gauge—it's only a ballpark figure. Everyone knits differently and with different tension, so your results will be unique.

Determining Yardage

Figuring out how much yarn you need is one of the more perplexing knitting decisions you'll make—you don't want to make a costly or inconvenient mistake. One way to take some of the anxiety out of the decision is to find a yarn shop which has a return policy for leftover balls. Another way is to relax and keep the extra yarn—build up a yarn stash to experiment with on a rainy day.

The following chart can help in your decision-making process. These are approximations based on averages taken from completed projects. You'll want to purchase enough yarn to complete your project using one dye-lot, to avoid making a garment with a mottled appearance or having another color line running through it.

You can also adjust the amounts using the following formulations:

For sleeveless styles, subtract 45%

For short sleeves, subtract 30%

For three-quarter-length sleeves, subtract 20%

For hip-length hem, add 20%

YARDAGE: LONG SLEEVE & JUST- ABOVE-HIP LENGTH*

Chest Size	S	M	L	XL
Actual body/in	32-34	36-38	40-42	44-46
Finished garment/in	34-36	38-40	42-44	46-48
Actual body /cm	80-85	90-95	100-105	110-115
Finished garment/cm	85-90	95-100	105-110	115-120

Gauge:				
2 sts/in	600	675	750	850
2.5	650	700	800	900
3	725	825	925	1075
3.5	875	1000	1125	1325
4	1020	1175	1300	1540
4.5	1140	1300	1475	1700
5	1275	1460	1660	1935
5.5	1400	1600	1800	2100

Projects

What's your style? Casual, open-front cardigan? A close-fitting pullover? A cosy turtleneck? Whichever you choose, you'll find a pattern here that suits your style and your knitting skill level. Better still, the patterns are arranged according to yarn type, featuring bulky, chunky, heavy worsted, and DK weight yarns. Pick your yarn and your pattern, and put your own personal stamp on it.

Cocoon

Here's a simple design that's perfect practice for learning how to make a semi-fitted sweater. The yoke is made the same way as for all other top-down sweaters, altering only slightly as you work the body downward. When working with bulky yarn, it's a good idea to slim the silhouette as much as possible, keeping a trim look and reducing the amount (and therefore the weight) of yarn on the body as well. The yarn stretches—hugs the hip—to accommodate the decreases that are taken in along the body sides.

experience level
Beginner

sizes
Small (Medium, Large, X-Large)

finished measurements
36 (40, 44, 48)"/91 (102, 112, 122)cm

materials
Approx total: 500(560, 586, 663)yd/457(512, 536, 607)m bulky weight yarn

Circular knitting needles (cn): 9 mm (size 13 U.S), one 29"/73cm and two 16"/40cm, *or size to obtain gauge*

Double-pointed needles (dpn): 9 mm (size 13 U.S), 10"/26cm, *or size to obtain gauge*

4 stitch markers

Tapestry needle

gauge
10 sts = 4"/10cm in St st

Always take time to check your gauge.

instructions

collar (work ITR)
Using 16"/40cm cn, CO 40 (42, 45, 48) sts.

Join and k for 8"/20cm.

yoke (work ITR)
Rnd 1: k16 (17, 19, 20) front sts, pm, k6 sleeve sts, pm, k12 (13, 14, 16) back sts, pm, k6 sleeve sts, pm.

Rnd 2 *(Inc rnd):* m1, * k to 1 st before marker, m1, sl marker, m1, repeat from * around for each marker, k around, end m1 (8 sts inc)—48 (50, 53, 56) sts.

Rnd 3: k.

Repeat Rnds 2 and 3, 13 (15, 17, 19) times more—152 (170, 189, 208) sts.

divide yoke (work ITR)
Separate body and sleeves:
Rnd 1: k44 (49, 55, 60) front sts, CO 2 (2, 1, 1) sts, pm, CO 1 st, place 34 (38, 42, 46) sleeve sts on 16"/40cm cn and *hold aside,* k40 (45, 50, 56) back sts,

CO 1 st, pm, CO 2 (2, 1, 1) sts, pm, place 34 (38, 42, 46) sleeve sts on 16"/40cm cn and *hold aside*—90 (100, 109, 120) sts on main cn.

body (work ITR)
K for 1"/2.5cm.

Next rnd: k2tog, k to next marker, sl marker, k2tog, k to end—88 (98, 107, 118) sts.

K 4 rnds.

Repeat last 5 rnds, 4 times more—80 (90, 99, 110) sts.

K until 11 1/2 (12 1/2, 13, 13)"/29 (32, 33, 33)cm from underarm to lower edge or desired length.

BO loosely.

sleeves (work ITR)
Using 34 (38, 42, 46) sts on 16"/40cm cn, pm at underarm:
Join and k for 1"/2.5cm.

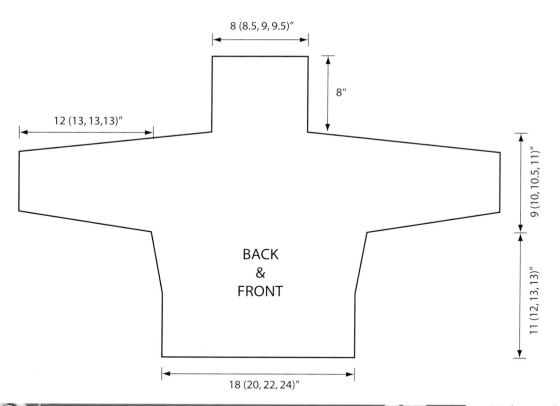

8 (8.5, 9, 9.5)"

8"

12 (13, 13,13)"

9 (10, 10.5, 11)"

11 (12, 13, 13)"

BACK
&
FRONT

18 (20, 22, 24)"

Underarm decreases; change to dpn as necessary:

Rnd 1: k2tog, k around, end k2tog—32 (36, 40, 44) sts.

K 4 (3, 3, 3) rnds.

Repeat last 5 (4, 4, 4) rnds, 5 (7, 8, 8) times more—22 (22, 24, 26) sts.

BO loosely.

Make second sleeve same as first.

finishing

Sew body and underarms together on each sleeve.

Using tapestry needle, weave in ends.

This project was made with:

10 (11, 12, 13) balls of Karabella's *Barbados*, 68% nylon/32% polyester, 1.75oz/50g = 51yd/47m, color #565 (green)

Aspen

Depending on the combination of yarn, tie, and sash trims used, you can achieve a wide range of looks with this belted cardigan. Try to decide which direction you'll take before you begin the sweater, making sure you coordinate all the elements. The belt holes can be eliminated entirely to make the cardigan hang straight. For a more casual look, add pockets either below or above the waistline, or in both places, mimicking a military/safari style.

instructions

collar (work B&F)

Using 16"/40cm cn, CO 32 (34, 36, 38) sts.

Rows 1–9: work k1/p1 rib.

Row 10 *(Inc row):* CO 2 sts (front band), work k1/p1 rib across, CO 2 sts (front band)—36 (38, 40, 42) sts.

yoke (work B&F)

Note: slip (sl) the first st of each row.

Row 1 (RS): sl 1, k7 (8, 8, 9) left front sts, pm, k5 sleeve sts, pm, k10 (10, 12, 12) back sts, pm, k5 sleeve sts, pm, k8 (9, 9, 10) right front sts.

Row 2 (WS): sl 1, k1, p across, end k2.

Row 3 (RS): sl 1, k1, * k to 1 st before next marker, m1, sl marker, m1, repeat from * across for each marker, k across, end k2 (8 sts inc)—44 (46, 48, 50) sts.

Row 4 (WS): sl 1, k1, p across, end k2.

Repeat Rows 3 and 4, 11 (12, 13, 15) times more.

divide yoke (work B&F)

Separate body and sleeves:

Row 1 (RS): sl 1, k1, work 19 (21, 22, 25) left front sts, place the 29 (31, 33, 37) sleeve sts on 16"/40cm cn and *hold aside,* CO 2 sts, k34 (36, 40, 44) back sts, CO 2 sts, place 29 (31, 33, 37) sleeve sts on 16"/40cm cn and *hold aside,* k20 (22, 23, 26) right front sts—78 (84, 90, 100) sts on main cn.

body (work B&F)

Work in St st, remembering to sl the first st in each row for 6 1/2 (6 3/4, 7, 7 1/2)"/16 (17, 18, 19)cm, or desired length to waistline.

eyelets for belt

Row 1 (RS): sl 1, k5 (5, 5, 6), BO 2 sts, * k7 (8, 9, 10), BO 2 sts, repeat from * across 7 times more, k to end.

Row 2 (WS): sl 1, k1, p across and CO 2 sts over each place where 2 sts were BO on previous row, end k2.

Work in St st for 5 (5 1/2, 6, 6 3/4)"/13 (14, 15, 17)cm.

hem
K 3 rows.
BO loosely.

sleeves (work ITR)
Using 29 (31, 33, 37) sts on 16"/40cm cn, pm at underarm:
m1, k around, end m1 (2 sts inc)—31 (33, 35, 39) sts.
Join and k for 1"/2.5cm.

Underarm sleeve dec; change to dpn as necessary:
Rnd 1: k2tog, k around, end k2tog (2 sts dec)—29 (31, 33, 37) sts.
K 3 (3, 3, 2) rnds.
Repeat last 4 (4, 4, 3) rnds, 6 (7, 7, 9) times more—17 (17, 19, 19) sts.

cuff
Rnd 1: k2tog, k around (1 st dec)—16 (16, 18, 18) sts.
Rnds 2–9: rib k1/p1.
Rnd 10: BO loosely.

Work second sleeve same as the first.

finishing
Sew body and underarms together on each sleeve.
Using tapestry needle, weave in ends.
Turn collar inward, double over, and slip stitch in place.

leather sash and neck tie
The sash can be made of a number of materials, including yarn I-cording, fabric (try an elongated scarf, or an old necktie, or two scarves or ties sewn together for length). You can also make your own belt out of lambskin hide, available through websites and online auctions. From the hide, cut out the sash; make two pieces of leather which, when hand-stitched together, measure 3 1/2"/9cm wide by a length three times your waist size. For the necktie, cut a piece that measures 3"/.9 m long by 2"/5cm wide. Weave the completed sash in and out of the belt-loop holes. For the necktie, attach a large safety pin to the end of the tie and use it to help you thread it through the tube collar. Cut fringe on the ends of the ties and sash only after they are in place.

This project was made with:

7 (8, 8, 9) balls of Karabella's *Puffy,* 100% wool, 3 1/2 oz/100g = approx 54yd/50m, color #1279 (brown rust)

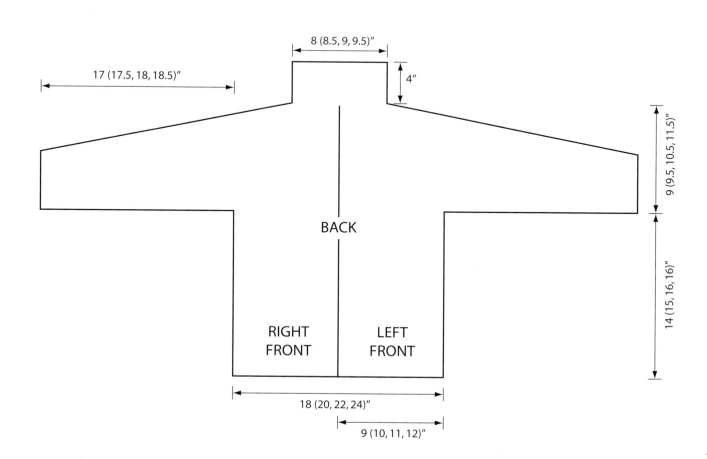

8 (8.5, 9, 9.5)"

17 (17.5, 18, 18.5)"

4"

9 (9.5, 10.5, 11.5)"

BACK

RIGHT FRONT

LEFT FRONT

14 (15, 16, 16)"

18 (20, 22, 24)"

9 (10, 11, 12)"

Sparks

There are so many fabulous, textured, novelty yarns available these days and one of the easiest and most stylish ways to use them is by making a very basic body shape, then adding a detail or two (such as the novelty yarn used for the cuffs and collar in this design). Depending on the yarn, this design looks just as good—or even better—on the reverse side, the way it's shown here.

instructions

collar (work ITR)
Using 16"/40cm cn and one strand each of yarns A and B held together, CO 40 (42, 45, 48) sts, pm.

Join and k for 3"/7.5cm.

yoke (work ITR)
Place markers:

Rnd 1: using A only, k16 (17, 19, 20) front sts, pm, k6 sleeve sts, pm, k12 (13, 14, 15) back sts, pm, k6 sleeve sts, pm.

Rnd 2 (*Inc rnd*): m1, * k to 1 st before next marker, m1, pm, m1, repeat from * for each marker, k until 1 st remains, m1 (8 sts inc)—48 (50, 53, 56) sts.

Rnd 3: k.

Repeat Rnds 2 and 3, 13 (15, 17, 19) times more.

divide yoke (work ITR)
Separate body and sleeves:

Rnd 1 (RS): k44 (49, 55, 60) front sts, CO 2 (2, 1, 1) sts, pm, CO 1 st, place 34 (38, 42, 46) sleeve sts on 16"/40cm cn and *hold aside*, k40 (45, 50, 56) back sts, CO 1 st, pm, CO 2 (2, 1, 1)

sts, place 34 (38, 42, 46) sleeve sts on 16"/40cm cn *and hold aside*—90 (100, 109, 120) sts on main cn.

body (work ITR)
K for 11 (12, 13, 14)"/28 (30, 32, 35)cm.

hem
P 3 rnds.

BO loosely.

sleeves
Using 34 (38, 42, 46) sts on 16"/40cm cn, pm at underarm:

K 0 (0, 2, 0) rnds.

Beg underarm sleeve dec, changing to dpn as necessary—join and work as follows:

Rnd 1: k2tog, k around, end k2tog (2 sts dec)—32 (36, 40, 44) sts.

K 5 (4, 4, 3) rnds.

Repeat last 6 (5, 5, 4) rnds, 6 (8, 9, 11) times more—20 (20, 22, 22) sts.

experience level
Beginner

sizes
Small (Medium, Large, X-Large)

fitted measurements
Bust 36 (40, 44, 48)"/91 (102, 112, 122)cm

materials
Approx total, yarn A: 490(530, 608, 675)yd/448(485, 556, 618)m bulky weight yarn

Approx total, yarn B: 70yd/64m bulky weight yarn

Circular needles (cn): 8 mm (size 11 U.S.), one 29"/73cm and two 16"/40cm, *or size to obtain gauge*

Double-pointed needles (dpn): 8 mm (size 11 U.S.), 10"/26cm, *or size to obtain gauge*

4 stitch markers

Tapestry needle

2 yd/1.8 m, 1"/2.5cm-wide ribbon

gauge
10 sts = 4"/10cm in St st

Always take time to check your gauge.

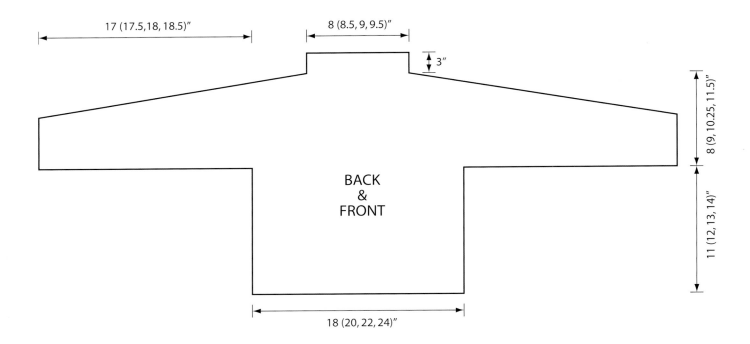

17 (17.5, 18, 18.5)"

8 (8.5, 9, 9.5)"

3"

8 (9, 10.25, 11.5)"

BACK
&
FRONT

11 (12, 13, 14)"

18 (20, 22, 24)"

cuff
Using yarns A and B held together:
K for 3"/7.5cm.
BO loosely.

finishing
Sew body and underarms together.
Using tapestry needle, weave in ends.

This project was made with:

A: 7 (7, 8, 9) balls of Classic Elite's
Rave, 42% mohair/31%
microfiber/27% poly, 1.75oz/50g =
approx 76yd/69m, color #7913
(black)

B: 1 ball of Bernat's *Boa*, 100% polyester, 1.75oz/50g = 71yd/56m, color
#81104 (mocking bird)

Verandah

This design is as classic as it gets. A boxy jacket can be easily paired with a skirt or pants, dressed up or down. It's easy to make, the only catch being that you'll have to make sure that the seed stitch pattern is maintained throughout, especially during transitions, such as when the yoke gets divided into the sleeves and front and back portions.

experience level
Intermediate

sizes
Small (Medium, Large, X-Large)

finished measurements
Bust 36 (40, 44, 48)"/91 (102, 112, 122)cm

materials
Approx total, yarn A: 450(475, 540, 585)yd/412 (435, 494, 535)m bulky weight yarn

Approx total, yarn B: 45yd/41m bulky weight yarn

Circular needles (cn): size 10 mm (15 U.S.), one 36"/91cm and two 16"/40cm, or size to obtain gauge

Double-pointed needles (dpn): 10 mm (size 15 U.S.) *or size to obtain gauge*

4 stitch markers

Tapestry needle

Crochet hook G or H

2 large buttons

gauge
8 sts = 4"/10cm in St st

Always take time to check your gauge.

pattern stitch
Seed Stitch (multiple of 2)
Rnd 1: *k1, p1, repeat from *
Rnd 2: *p1, k1, repeat from *
Rep Rnds 1 and 2.

instructions

collar (work B&F)

Note: sl the first st of each row.

Using 29"/73cm cn and yarn A, CO 32 (34, 36, 38) sts.

Row 1: sl 1, k to end.

Row 2: rep Row 1.

yoke (work B&F)

Note: the first 2 sts of each side are worked in garter stitch for front band throughout.

Row 1 (RS): sl 1, k6 (6, 7, 7) left front sts, pm, k5 sleeve sts, pm, k8 (10, 10, 12) back sts, pm, k5 sleeve sts, pm, k7 (7, 8, 8) right front sts.

Row 2 (WS): sl 1, k1, * work seed st until 1 st before marker, p1, sl marker, p1, repeat from * for each subsequent marker, work seed st, end k2.

Row 3 (RS): sl 1, k1, * work seed stitch to 1 st before first marker, t1, sl marker, k1, t1, repeat from * for each subsequent marker, work seed st across, end k2 (8 sts inc).

Rep Rows 2 and 3, 11 (12, 13, 15) times more—128 (138, 148, 166) sts.

divide yoke (work B&F)

Separate body and sleeves:

Row 1 (RS): sl 1, k1, work 17 (18, 20, 22) left front sts in pat, CO 1 (1, 2, 1) sts, pm, CO 0 (1, 1, 1), place 29 (31, 33, 37) sleeve sts on 16"/40cm cn and *hold aside,* k32 (36, 38, 44) back sts, CO 0 (1, 1, 1), pm, CO 1 (1, 2, 1), place 29 (31, 33, 37) sleeve sts on 16"/40cm cn and *hold aside,* work 17 (18, 20, 22) sts in pat, end k2 sts.

body (work B&F)

Work in pat for 10 (11, 12, 12)"/25 (28, 31, 31)cm—*remember to sl the first st in each row and keep the 2 st of the front bands in garter st.*

hem

K 2 rnds.

BO loosely.

sleeves (work ITR)

Using 29 (31, 33, 37) sleeve sts on 16"/40cm cn, pm at underarm, changing to dpn as necessary:

Join and work in pat for 1"/2.5cm.

Next rnd: K2tog, work in pat across, end k2tog.

Work 4 rnds in pat.

Repeat last 5 rnds, 5 (6, 6, 6) times more—16 (18, 20, 20) sts.

Work pat until desired sleeve length.

cuff

K 1 rnd.

P 1 rnd.

BO loosely.

Work second sleeve same as the first.

finishing

Sew body and underarms together on each sleeve.

Using tapestry needle, weave in ends.

cuff decoration

Thread a tapestry needle with yarn B. Using a doubled strand, weave the yarn in and out of the raised seed of the seed st along the 4 bottom rows of the cuff.

tie (make 2)

Using the crochet hook and yarn B, make a 12"/31cm-long chain. Fasten off. Attach each tie to front neck edge. On either side of top neckline, sew a large button over the spot where the tie is attached.

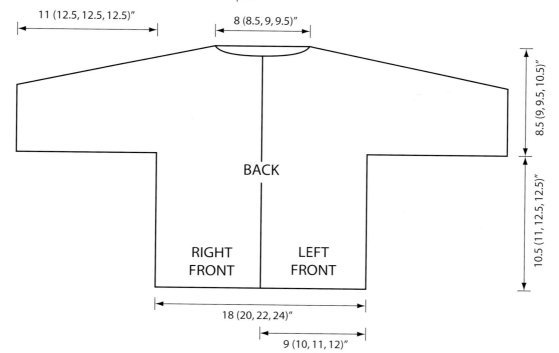

Luscious bulky yarns are so tempting to use because they work up quickly. Care has to be taken, though, to eliminate excess bulk. Streamline the shape by minimizing body shape and details. Here a simple collar and three-quarter-length sleeve is used.

instructions

collar (work B&F)
Using 29"/73cm cn, CO 32 (34, 36, 38) sts.

K for 1"/2.5cm.

yoke (work B&F)
Row 1 (RS): s1, k5 (6, 6, 7) left front sts, pm, k5 sleeve sts, pm, k10 (10, 12, 12) back sts, pm, k5 sleeve sts, pm, k6 (7, 7, 8) right front sts.

Row 2 (WS): s1, k across.

Row 3 (RS): s1 *k to 1 st before marker, m1, slip marker, m1, repeat from * across for each subsequent marker, k to end (8 sts inc)—40 (42, 44, 46) sts.

Rep Rows 2 and 3, 5 (5, 6, 6) times more—80 (82, 92, 94) sts.

K 1 row.

join yoke (work ITR)
Pm on right-hand needle denoting middle front:

Rnd 1 (RS): *k to 1 st before marker, m1, slip marker, m1, repeat from * across for each subsequent marker, k to end (middle marker) (8 sts inc)—88 (90, 100, 102) sts.

Rnd 2: k 1 rnd.

Rep last two rounds 5 (6, 6, 8) times more—128 (138, 148, 166) sts.

Next rnd: k around to beg of *front sts* (4th marker—not the middle front, 5th marker, where the body and work ITR began).

divide yoke (work ITR)
Separate body and sleeve sts:

Rnd 1 (RS): k36 (40, 42, 48) front sts, CO 1, pm, CO 0 (1, 2, 1), place 29 (31, 33, 37) sleeve sts on 16"/40cm cn and *hold aside*, k34 (36, 40, 44) back sts, CO 0 (1, 2, 1), pm, CO 1, place 29 (31, 33, 37) sleeve sts on second 16"/40cm cn and *hold aside*—72 (80, 88, 96) sts on main cn.

body (work ITR)
With sts on main cn:

K for 7 (8, 9, 9)"/18 (20, 23, 23)cm.

hem
P 1 rnd.

K 1 rnd.

Rep last 2 rnds 4 times more.

BO loosely.

experience level
Intermediate

sizes
Small (Medium, Large, X-Large)

finished measurements
Bust 36 (40, 44, 48)"/91 (102, 112, 122)cm

materials
Approx total: 460(474, 520, 560) yd/421(434, 476, 512)m bulky weight yarn

Circular knitting needles (cn): 10 mm (size 15 U.S.), one 29"/73cm and two 16"/40cm, *or size to obtain gauge*

Double-pointed needles (dpn): 10 mm (size 15 U.S.) *or size to obtain gauge*

5 stitch markers

Tapestry needle

gauge
8 sts = 4"/10cm in St st

Always take time to check your gauge.

notes
This pattern begins like a cardigan in that you need to work back and forth on a circular needle to create the split yoke. Then it takes the form of a pullover when the yoke is joined and worked ITR.

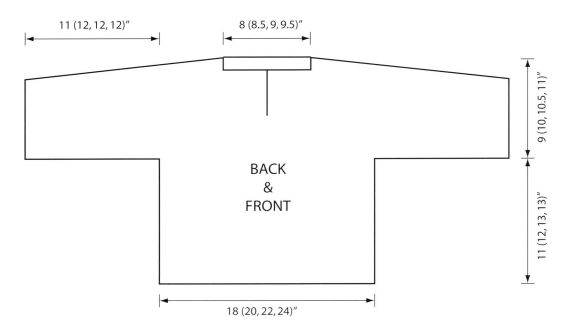

11 (12, 12, 12)"

8 (8.5, 9, 9.5)"

9 (10, 10.5, 11)"

BACK
&
FRONT

11 (12, 13, 13)"

18 (20, 22, 24)"

sleeves (work ITR)

*Using 29 (31,33,37) sts on 16"/40cm
cn, changing to dpn as necessary:*
K for 8 (9, 9, 9)"/20 (23, 23, 23)cm.

cuff

P 1 rnd.

K 1 rnd.

Rep last 2 rnds, 4 times more.

BO loosely.

Work second sleeve same as the first.

finishing

Sew body and underarms together on each sleeve.

With tapestry needle, weave in ends.

This project was made with:

14 (15, 16, 17) balls of Rowan's *Big Wool*, 100% wool, 3.5oz/100g = approx 33yd/30m per ball, color #243 (cookie)

$\mathcal{B}$irch

This classic turtleneck, made more interesting with a textured yarn, is a great beginner project. It's so easy to make that you could whip it up overnight and wear it on the ski slopes the next day!

experience level
Beginner

sizes
Small (Medium, Large, X-Large)

finished measurements
Bust 36 (40, 44, 48)"/91 (102, 112, 122)cm

materials
Approx total: 650(690, 720, 775)yd/595 (631, 659, 709)m bulky weight yarn

Circular needles (cn): 9 mm (size 13 U.S.), one 29"/73cm and two 16"/40cm, *or size to obtain gauge*

Double-pointed needles (dpn): 4.5 mm (size U.S.), 10"/25cm, *or size to obtain gauge*

4 stitch markers

Tapestry needle

gauge
10 sts = 4"/10cm

Always take time to check your gauge.

instructions

turtleneck (work ITR)

Using 16"/40cm cn, CO 40 (42, 45, 48) sts.

Work k1/p1 rib for 7"/18cm.

yoke (work ITR)

Rnd 1 (RS): k16 (17, 19, 20) front sts, pm, k6 shoulder sts, pm, k12 (13, 14, 16) back sts, pm, k6 shoulder sts, pm.

Rnd 2 (Inc rnd): m1, *k to 1 st before next marker, m1, sl m, m1, repeat from * around 3 times more, k around, end m1 (8 sts inc)—48 (50, 52, 56) sts.

Rnd 3: k.

Repeat Rnds 2 and 3, 13 (15, 17, 19) times more—152 (170, 189, 208) sts

K 1 rnd.

divide yoke (work ITR)

Separate body and sleeves:

Rnd 1 (RS): k44 (49, 55, 60) front sts, CO 2 (2, 1, 1) sts, pm, CO 1 st, place 34 (38, 42, 46) sleeve sts on 16"/40cm cn and hold aside, k40 (45, 50, 56) back sts, CO 1 st, pm, CO 2(2, 1, 1), place 34 (38, 42, 46) sleeve sts on 16"/40cm cn and hold aside—90 (100,109, 120) body sts remain on cn.

body (work ITR)

Joining front and back parts:

k for 11 (12, 12 1/2, 12 1/2)"/27 (30, 31, 31)cm.

hem

Work k1/p1 rib for 2.5"/6cm.

BO loosely in rib.

sleeves

Using 34 (38, 42, 46) sts on 16"/40cm cn and switching to dpn as necessary:

Rnd 1 (RS): Join and k around, CO 1 st, pm at underarm, CO 1 st (2 sts inc)—36 (40, 44, 48) sts.

K 8 (8, 6, 0) rnds.

Beg sleeve dec:

Rnd 1: k2tog, k around, end k2tog (2 sts dec)—34 (38, 42, 46) sts.

K 4 (3, 3, 3) rnds.

Repeat last 5 (4, 4, 4) rnds, 6 (8, 9, 11) times more—20 (20, 22, 22) sts.

cuff

Work k1/p1 rib for 3"/7.5cm.

BO loosely.

finishing

Sew underarms together and weave in ends.

This project was made with:

4 (4, 4, 5) balls of Classic Elite's *Tigress*, 100% wool, 200g = 181yd/165m, color #7016 (white tiger)

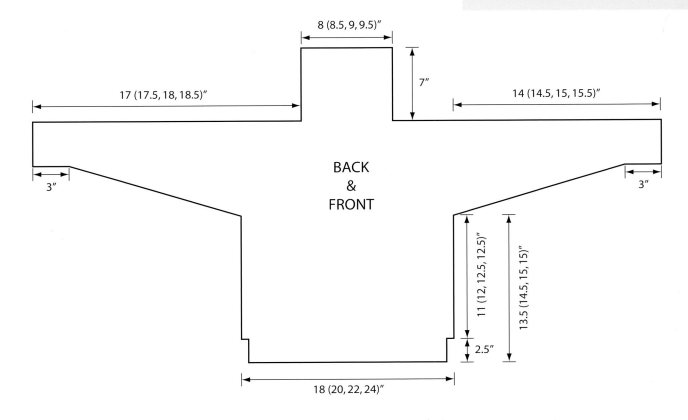

8 (8.5, 9, 9.5)"

7"

17 (17.5, 18, 18.5)"

14 (14.5, 15, 15.5)"

3"   3"

BACK
&
FRONT

11 (12, 12.5, 12.5)"

13.5 (14.5, 15, 15)"

2.5"

18 (20, 22, 24)"

New leaf

An homage to k2/p2 ribbing, this design features the ribbing for the neckline, extended cuffs, and body of the sweater. The basic, chunky-weight pullover pattern (see page 117) was adjusted to accommodate the 4-stitch-multiple required for a 2/2 rib pattern. The result is a stylish, fitted pullover that's as easy to wear as it is to make.

experience level
Beginner

sizes
Small (Medium, Large, X-Large)

finished measurements
Bust 36 (40, 44, 48)"/91 (102, 112, 122)cm

materials
Approx total: 654(709, 870, 980)yd/598(649, 795, 897)m chunky weight yarn

Circular knitting needles (cn): 6 mm (size 10 U.S.), one 29"/73cm and two 16"/40cm, *or size to obtain gauge*

Double-pointed needles (dpn): 6 mm (size 10 U.S.) *or size to obtain gauge*

4 stitch markers

Tapestry needle

gauge
12 sts = 4"/20cm in St st

Always take time to check your gauge.

instructions

collar (work ITR)
Using 16"/40cm cn, CO 48 (52, 56, 56) sts.

Rnds 1–5: Join sts and rib k2/p2.

Rnd 6: k, inc 0 (dec 1, dec 2, inc 1) sts evenly spaced—48 (51, 54, 57) sts.

yoke (work ITR)
Rnd 1 (RS): k19 (21, 22, 24) front sts, pm, k8 sleeve sts, pm, k13 (14, 16, 17) back sts, pm, k8 sleeve sts, pm.

Rnd 2: m1, * k to 1 st before next marker, m1, slm, m1, repeat from * around for each marker, k, end, m1 (8 sts inc)—56 (59, 62, 65) sts.

Rnd 3: k.

Repeat Rnds 2 and 3, 17 (19, 21, 23) times more—192 (211, 230, 249) sts.

divide yoke (work ITR)
Separate body and sleeves:

Rnd 1 (RS): k55 (61, 66, 72) front sts, CO 1 (1, 2, 2) sts, pm, CO 1 (1, 1, 2) sts, place 44 (48, 52, 56) sleeve sts on 16"/40cm cn and *hold aside*, k49 (54, 60, 65) back sts, CO 1 st, pm, CO 1 (2, 2, 2) sts, place 44 (48, 52, 56) sleeve sts on 16"/40cm cn and *hold aside*—108 (120, 132, 144) sts on main cn.

body (work ITR)
Rnds 1–6: k.

Work k2/p2 rib for 11 (11, 12, 13)"/28 (28, 30, 33)cm from underarm.

BO loosely in rib.

sleeves (work ITR)
Using 44 (48, 52, 56) sleeve sts on 16"/40cm cn, join and work as follows, switching to dpn as necessary:

Rnd 1: k around, CO 1 st, pm, CO 1 st (2 sts inc)—46 (50, 54, 58) sts.

K 5 rnds.

Begin underarm sleeve dec, changing to dpn as needed:

Rnd 1: k2tog, k around, end k2tog (2 sts dec)—44 (48, 52, 56) sts.

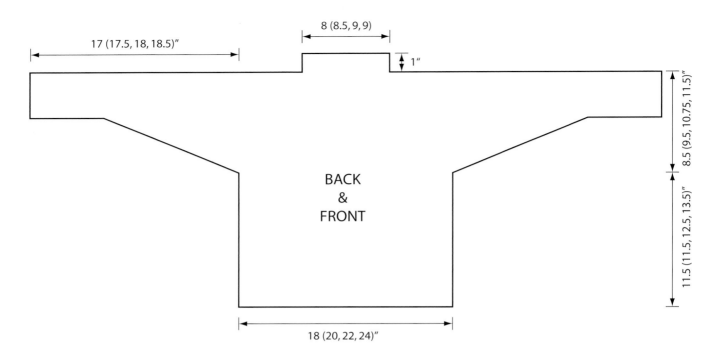

BACK
&
FRONT

8 (8.5, 9, 9)"

17 (17.5, 18, 18.5)"

1"

8.5 (9.5, 10.75, 11.5)"

11.5 (11.5, 12.5, 13.5)"

18 (20, 22, 24)"

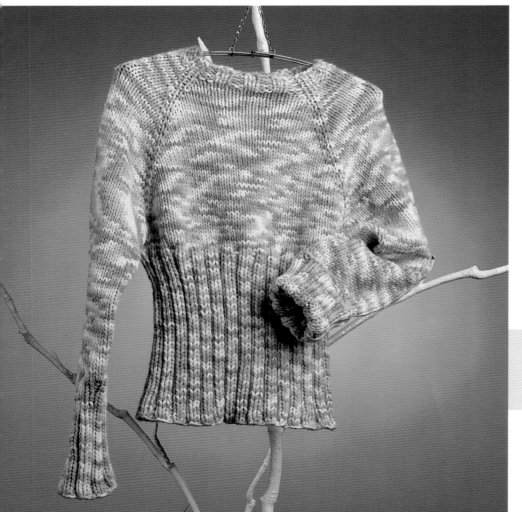

Rnds 2–4: k 3 rnds.

Repeat Rnds 1–4, 4 (4, 6, 6) times more—36 (40, 40, 44) sts.

cuff

Work k2/p2 rib until sleeve measures 17 (17 1/2, 18, 18 1/2)"/43 (44, 46, 47)cm from underarm or desired length.

BO loosely.

Work second sleeve same as the first.

finishing

Sew body and underarms together on each sleeve.

Using tapestry needle, weave in ends.

This project was made with:

6 (7, 8, 9) balls of Classic Elite's *Paintbox,* 100% wool, 1.75oz/50g = approx 109yd/100m, color #6897 (watercolor green)

Indian summer

Here, the capelet, or extended cowl collar, provides the drama. For added dash, you can make it even longer just by lengthening it—keep knitting! The body of the sweater is just an understated pullover with a ribbed cuff hem—a simple detail that results in a more polished look.

experience level
Beginner

sizes
Small (Medium, Large, X-Large)

finished measurements
Bust: 36 (40, 44, 48)"/91 (102, 112, 122)cm

materials
- Approx total: 600(695, 780, 870)yd/549(636, 714, 795)m chunky weight yarn
- Circular knitting needles (cn): 4.5 mm (size 7 U.S.), one 29"/73cm and two 16"/40cm, or size *to obtain gauge*
- Double-pointed needles (dpn): 4.5 mm (size 7 U.S.) 10"/25cm
- 4 stitch markers
- Tapestry needle

gauge
12 sts = 4"/10cm in St st

Always take time to check your gauge.

instructions

collar (work ITR)

Using 16"/40cm cn, CO 112 (120, 136, 144) sts.

Join and rib k4/p4 for 5"/12.5cm.

Next rnd: * k1, k2tog, k1, p1, p2tog, p1, repeat from * around—84 (90, 102, 108) sts.

Work 4 rnds, knitting the k sts and purling the p sts.

Next rnd: * k1, k2tog, p1, p2tog, repeat from * around—56 (60, 68, 72) sts.

Next rnd: k, dec 8 (9, 14, 15) sts evenly around—48 (51, 54, 57) sts.

yoke (work ITR)

Rnd 1: k19 (21, 22, 24) front sts, pm, k8 sleeve sts, pm, k13 (14, 16, 17) back sts, pm, k8 sleeve sts, pm.

Rnd 2 (Inc rnd): m1, *k to 1 st before next marker, m1, sl marker, m1, repeat from * for each subsequent marker, k around, end m1 (8 sts inc)—56 (59, 62, 65) sts.

Rnd 3: k.

Repeat Rnds 2 and 3, 17 (19, 21, 23) times more—192 (211, 230, 249) sts.

divide yoke (work ITR)

Separate body and sleeve sts:

Rnd 1: k55 (61, 66, 72) front sts, CO 1 (1, 2, 2) sts, pm, CO 1 st, place 44 (48, 52, 56) sleeve sts on 16"/40cm cn and *hold aside*, k49 (54, 60, 65) back sts, CO 1 st, pm, CO 1 (1, 2, 2) sts, place 44 (48, 52, 56) sleeve sts on 16"/40cm cn and *hold aside*—108 (119, 132, 143) sts on main cn.

body (work ITR)

K for 9 (10, 11, 11 1/2)"/22.5 (25, 27 1/2, 29)cm.

hem

Rnd 1: k, inc 4 (inc 1, dec 4, inc 1) st(s) evenly around—112 (120, 128, 144) sts.

Rib k4/p4 for 4"/10cm.

BO in rib.

sleeves (work ITR)

Using 44 (48, 52, 56) sleeve sts on the 16"/40cm cn:

k around, CO 1 st, pm, CO 1 st.

K for 1"/ 2.5cm.

Underarm decreases; change to dpns as necessary:

Rnd 1: k2tog, k until 2 sts before end, k2tog—(2 st dec)—42 (46, 50, 54) sts.

K 5 (5, 4, 4) rnds.

Repeat last 6 (6, 5, 5) rnds, 8 (9, 11, 12) times more—28 (30, 30, 32) sts.

Work even, if necessary, until sleeve measures 14 (14 1/2, 15, 15 1/2)"/36 (37, 38, 40)cm.

cuff

Work k1/p1 rib for 2"/5cm.

BO loosely.

Work second sleeve same as the first.

finishing

Sew body and underarms together on each sleeve.

Using tapestry needle, weave in ends.

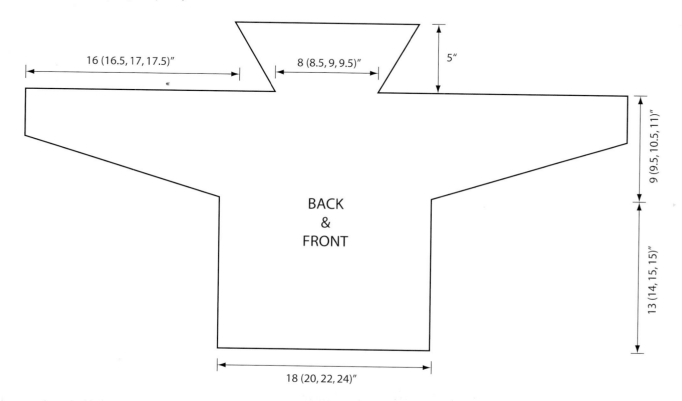

16 (16.5, 17, 17.5)"

8 (8.5, 9, 9.5)"

5"

9 (9.5, 10.5, 11)"

13 (14, 15, 15)"

BACK & FRONT

18 (20, 22, 24)"

&vergreen

It took a while to figure out what kind of ribbing to use for this collar. Initially, I wanted to go with a k2/p2 rib, to create an undulating pattern. But when I started a sample with the yarn of my choice, I realized that its heft might overwhelm the collar structure, so I went with a k1/p1 rib instead. That's the advantage of top-down knitting—you can think through the design each step of the way to accommodate the type of yarn you want to use and adjust for style considerations.

instructions

collar (work B&F)
Using 16"/40cm cn and yarn B, CO 96 (102, 108, 114) sts.

Work k1/p1 rib for 6"/15cm.

K2tog across—48 (51, 54, 57) sts.

P 1 row.

Eyelet row: k4, * yo, k2tog, repeat from * across, end k4 (3, 4, 4) sts.

P 1 row.

yoke (work ITR)
Note: slip (sl) the first st in each row along the front band and keep 5 sts on either side in garter st for front bands.

Using yarn A:

Rnd 1 (RS): sl 1, k8 (9, 10, 11) left front sts, pm, k8 sleeve sts, pm, k14 (15, 16, 17) back sts, pm, k8 sleeve sts, pm, k9 (10, 11, 12) right front sts.

Rnd 2 (WS): sl 1, k4 (front band), p across, end k5 (front band).

Rnd 3 (RS): sl 1, * k to 1 st before marker, m1, sl marker, m1, repeat from * around for each marker, k to end (8

sts inc)—56 (59, 62, 65) sts.

Rnd 4 (WS): sl 1, k4, p across, end k5.

Repeat Rnds 3 and 4, 17 (19, 21, 23) times more.

divide yoke (work ITR)
Separate body and sleeves:

Row 1 (RS): k27 (30, 33, 36) left front sts, CO 1 (1, 2, 2) sts, pm, CO 1 st, place 44 (48, 52, 56) sleeve sts on 16"/40cm cn and *hold aside*, k50 (55, 60, 65) back sts, CO 1 st, pm, CO 1 (1, 2, 2) sts, place 44 (48, 52, 56) sleeve sts on 16"/40cm cn and *hold aside*, k27 (30, 33, 36) right front sts—108 (119, 132, 143) sts.

body (work B&F)
Work St st for 10 (11, 12, 12)"/25 (28, 31, 31)cm, keeping 5 sts at front edges in garter st.

hem
k for 1"/2.5cm.

BO loosely.

experience level
Intermediate

size
Small (Medium, Large, X-Large)

finished measurements
Bust 38 (40, 44, 48)"/91 (100, 110, 120)cm

materials
Approx total, yarn A: 492(574, 656, 738)yd/450(525, 600, 675)m chunky weight yarn

Approx total, yarn B: 220yd/202m chunky weight yarn

Approx total, yarn C: 110yd/101m chunky weight yarn

Circular needles (cn): 6.5 mm (size 10 1/2 U.S.), one 29"/73cm and two 16"/40cm, *or size to obtain gauge*

Double-pointed needles (dpn): 6.5 mm (size 10 1/2 U.S.), 10"/26cm, *or size to obtain gauge*

4 stitch markers

Crochet hook size H/8 U.S.

Tapestry needle

gauge
12 sts = 4"/10cm in St st

Always take time to check your gauge.

sleeves (work ITR)

Using 44 (48, 52, 56) sleeve sts on 16"/40cm cn:

CO 1 st, pm, CO 1 st (2 sts inc)—46 (50, 54, 58) sts.

Join and k for 1"/2.5cm.

Beg underarm sleeve dec, changing to dpn as needed:

Rnd 1: k2tog, k around, end k2tog (2 sts dec)—44 (48, 52, 56).

Repeat Rnd 1 every 1"/2.5cm, 8 (10, 10, 12) times—30 (30, 34, 34) sts.

K until sleeve measures 11 (11 1/2, 12, 12 1/2)"/28 (27, 27, 32)cm from underarm.

cuff

Using yarn B, rib k1/p1 for 6"/15cm. BO loosely.

Work second sleeve same as the first.

finishing

Sew body and underarms together on each sleeve.

Using tapestry needle, weave in ends.

Make six 1"/2.5cm pom-poms: 4 in yarn C and 2 in yarn B.

collar lacings

Using the crochet hook and one strand of yarn C, chain two ties, one 38"/95cm and one 39"/98cm. With yarn B, chain one tie 40"/100cm. Start each chain by leaving a 8"/20cm tail and end each chain leaving the same— these tails will be used to tie on the pom-poms. Using a tapestry needle, string the pom-pom on the end of a matching lacing and secure; do the same with the other lacings. With the three lacings of the non-pom-pom ends, thread the three strands of yarn together, then weave the set of lacings through the lacing holes that were made just below the collar. Once they have been eased in and adjusted, secure the three remaining pom-poms on the opposite ends.

This project was made with:

A: 6 (7, 8, 9) balls of Lion Brand's *Moonlight Mohair*, 57% acrylic/28% mohair, 1.75 oz/50g = approx 82yd/50m, color #211 (everglades)

B: 2 balls of Reynold's *Lopi*, 100% wool, 3.5oz/100g = approx 110yd/101m, color #9983 (light olive)

C: 1 ball of Reynold's *Lopi*, 100% wool, 3.5oz/100g = approx 110yd/101m, color #9965 (yellow/green)

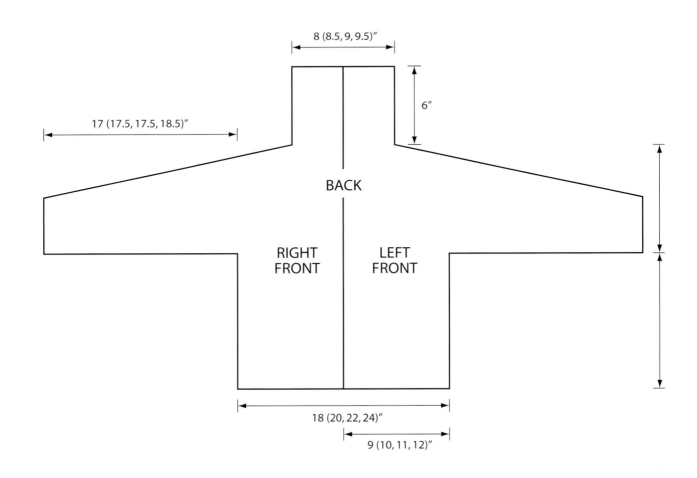

Hyacinth

This sweater would look good in any number of color combinations. Pairing texture (bobbles) with tonal yarns in cool colors has a striking effect. The twisted rib cuffs, hem, and collar also go beyond the ordinary k1/p1 rib for an added dimension. Making the bobble yoke does take a bit of time, but the rest of the sweater works up quickly.

experience level
Intermediate

sizes
Small (Medium, Large, X-Large)

finished measurements
Bust 36 (40, 44, 48)"/91 (102, 112, 122)cm

materials
- Approx total, yarn A: 500(550, 660, 820)yd/460(503, 604, 750)m chunky weight yarn
- Approx total, 7 different stripe colors (SC): 70 yd/64m each chunky weight yarn
- Circular knitting needles (cn): 6 mm (size 10 U.S.), one 29"/73cm and two 16"/40cm, or size to obtain gauge
- Double-pointed needles (dpn): 6 mm (size 10 U.S.) or size to obtain gauge
- 4 stitch markers
- Tapestry needle

gauge
14 sts = 4"/10cm in St st

Always take time to check your gauge.

notes
Make Bobble (MB)
Making a bobble requires that you knit into a stitch 6 times, pulling up the new sts, starting at the back of the st and alternating to the front. You will end up with a cluster of sts on the right-hand needle. Then, starting with the outer-most st on the right side of the cluster, pull that st over all the others, dropping it as you go, and repeat this with every subsequent st until only 1 st remains. Slip this last st onto the left-hand needle and knit it—voilà! As arduous as this may seem the first time you do it, it actually becomes second nature as you move along.

instructions

collar (work ITR)

Using yarn A and 16"/40cm cn, CO 54 (56, 56, 60) sts.

Join and work twisted k1/p1 rib (knit the k sts through the back loop) for 3"/5cm.

Next rnd: k, inc 2 (3, 7, 6) sts evenly around—56 (59, 63, 66) sts.

yoke (work ITR)

Rnd 1: With A, k23 (25, 27, 28) front sts, pm, k8 sleeve sts, pm, k17 (18, 20, 22) sts, pm, k8 sleeve sts, pm.

Bobble rnd—using a combination of two contrasting colors, one for the background (SC1) and one for the bobble (SC2):

Rnd 1: * k3 with SC1, MB with SC2, repeat from * around.

Rnd 2 (Inc rnd): with SC1, m1, * k to 1 st before next marker, m1, sl marker, m1, repeat from * around for each subsequent marker, k around, end m1 (8 sts inc)—64 (67, 71, 74) sts.

Rnd 3: with SC1, k.

Rnd 4: repeat Rnd 2 (8 sts inc)—72 (75, 79, 82) sts.

Next rnds: using two different colors for SC1 and SC2 for each 4-rnd section, repeat Rnds 1 through 4, 7 (9, 10, 10) times more.

Bobble rnd—using A and another contrasting color for the bobble (SC2):

Rnd 1: * k3 with A, MB with SC2, repeat from * around.

With A only:

Rnd 2 (Inc rnd): m1, * k to 1 st before next marker, m1, sl marker, m1, repeat from * around for each subsequent marker, k around, end m1 (8 sts inc)—192 (227, 247, 258) sts.

Rnd 3: k.

Rep Rnds 2 and 3, 3 (2, 3, 4) times more for a total of 20 (23, 26, 27) inc rnds on yoke)—216 (243, 271, 290) sts.

divide yoke (work ITR)

Separate body and sleeves:

Rnd 1: with A, k63 (71, 79, 84) front sts, CO 1 (1, 1, 2) sts, pm, CO 1 st, place 48 (54, 60, 64) sleeve sts on 16"40cm cn and *hold aside,* k57 (64, 72, 78) back sts, CO 1 st, pm, CO 2 (1, 1, 1) sts, place 48 (54, 60, 64) sleeve sts on 16"/40cm cn and *hold aside,* pm—124 (139, 155, 168) sts on main cn.

body (work ITR)

Using A only:

K for 9 (10, 11, 11 1/2)"/22 (25, 27, 29)cm.

hem

Work twisted k1/p1 rib for 3"/8cm.

BO loosely in twisted rib.

sleeves (work ITR)

With A and using 16"/40cm cn, k48 (54, 60, 64) sts on cn, switch to dpn as necessary:

Rnd 1: CO 1 st, pm, CO 1 st, k to end (2 sts inc)—50 (56, 62, 66) sts.

K for 1 1/2"/4cm.

Underarm sleeve dec:

K2tog, work around, end k2tog (2 sts dec)—48 (54, 60, 64) sts.

Work 6 (4, 4, 3) rnds.

Repeat last 7 (5, 5, 4) rnds, 7 (10, 11, 13) times more—32 (32, 36, 36) sts.

Work until sleeve measures 13 (13 3/4, 13 3/4, 14)"/33 (35, 35, 36)cm from underarm.

Bobble rnd—using one color for the background (SC1), another for the bobble (SC2):

Rnd 1: * k3 with SC1, MB with SC2, repeat from * around.

Rnd 2: with SC1, k2tog, k around, end k2tog—30 (30, 34, 34) sts.

Rnds 3 and 4: with SC1, k.

Using a different set of colors for SC1 and SC2:

Rnds 5–8: rep Rnds 1–4 (2 sts dec)—28 (28, 32, 32) sts.

Final bobble rnd—using A for background and a contrasting color (SC2) for the bobble:

Rnd 1: * k3 with A, MB with SC2, repeat from * around.

Rnds 2–3: With A, k.

cuff

Work twisted k1/p1 rib for 2"/5cm.

BO loosely in twisted rib.

finishing

Sew body and underarms together on each sleeve.

Using tapestry needle, weave in ends.

Fold collar in half inward and baste loosely to inner edge.

This project was made with:

A: 5 (5, 6, 7) balls of Reynold's *Lopi*, 100% wool, 3.5oz/100g = approx 110yd/101m in #308 (aqua)

SCs: 1 ball each of Reynold's *Lopi*, 100% wool, 3.5oz/100g = approx 110yd/101m, in colors #390 (hyacinth violet), #378 (leaf green), #9982 (lake blue), #82 (cornflower), #9983 (green apple), #301 (grass green), and #214 (bright blue teal)

experience level
Easy

sizes
Small (Medium, Large, X-Large)

finished measurements
Bust 38 (40, 44, 48)"/91 (100, 110, 120)cm

materials
Approx total: 775(850, 925, 1000)yd/709 (778, 846, 915)m chunky weight yarn

Circular needles (cn): 6 mm (size 10 U.S.), one 29"/73cm and two 16"/40cm, *or size to obtain gauge*

Double-pointed needles (dpn): 6 mm (size 10 U.S.), 10"/25cm, *or size to obtain gauge*

4 stitch markers

Tapestry needle

gauge
14 sts = 4"/20cm in garter st

Always take time to check your gauge.

pattern stitch
Garter stitch (work B&F): k every row.

Garter stitch (work ITR): k 1 rnd, p 1 rnd.

Flora

Polo collars frame any face nicely, and they are very easy to execute. Cast on the required number of neckline stitches and knit to the desired length. To finish, three-quarter-length sleeves are versatile, practical, and universally flattering.

instructions

collar (work B&F)
Using 29"/73cm cn, CO 56 (59, 63, 66) sts.

Work garter st for 4"/10cm, slipping the first st in each row.

yoke (work B&F)
Note: sl the first st of each row.

Row 1 (RS): sl 1, k 10 (11, 12, 13) left front sts, pm, k8 sleeve sts, pm, k18 (19, 21, 22) back sts, pm, k8 sleeve sts, pm, k11 (12, 13, 14) right front sts.

Row 2 (WS): sl 1, k across.

Row 3 (RS): sl 1, * k to 1 st before marker, m1, sl marker, m1, repeat from * across for each marker, k across, (8 sts inc)—64 (67, 71, 74) sts.

Repeat Rows 2 and 3, 19 (22, 25, 27) times more—216 (243, 271, 290) sts.

divide yoke (work B&F)
Separate body and sleeves:

Row 1 (RS): sl 1, k30 (34, 38, 41) left front sts, CO 1 (1, 1, 2) sts, pm, CO 1 st, place 48 (54, 60, 64) sleeve sts on 16"/40cm cn and *hold aside*, k58 (65, 73, 78) back sts, CO 1 st, pm, CO 1 (1, 1, 2) sts, place 48 (54, 60, 64) sleeve sts on 16"/40cm cn and *hold aside*, k31 (35, 39, 42) right front sts— 124 (139, 155, 168) sts on main cn.

body (work B&F)
K for 11 (12, 12, 13)"/27 (30, 30, 32)cm, slipping the first st in each row. BO loosely.

sleeves (work ITR)
Using 48 (54, 60, 64) sleeve sts on 16"/40cm cn:

CO 1 st, pm, CO 1 st at underarm— 50 (56, 62, 66) sts.

Join and work garter st for 1"/2.5cm (see note, left, for how to make garter st ITR), ending completing a p rnd.

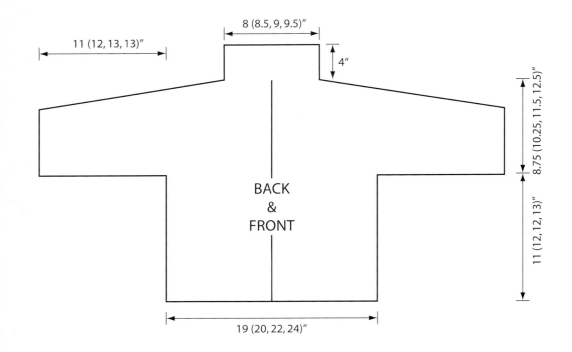

8 (8.5, 9, 9.5)"

11 (12, 13, 13)"

4"

8.75 (10.25, 11.5, 12.5)"

BACK
&
FRONT

11 (12, 12, 13)"

19 (20, 22, 24)"

Underarm sleeve decs; change to dpn as necessary:

Rnd 1 *(Dec rnd):* k2tog, k around, end k2tog (2 sts dec)—48 (54, 60, 64) sts.

Work 4 rnds in garter st.

Repeat Rnds 1 through 5, 5 (6, 8, 8) times more—38 (42, 44, 48) sts.

Work until sleeve measures 11 1/2 (12 1/2, 13 1/2, 13 1/2)"/29 (31, 34, 34)cm or desired length.

BO loosely.

Work second sleeve same as the first.

finishing

Sew body and underarms together on each sleeve.

Using tapestry needle, weave in ends.

This project was made with:

11 (11, 12, 13) balls of Muench's *Oceana,* 55% viscose/30% nylon/15% cotton, 1.75oz/50g = approx 77yd/70m, color #4806 (green)

Dewdrop

Before attempting this design, you'll need to understand the basic concept of how a standard cardigan is done in the top-down technique. This variation employs a bit more shaping. If you're somewhat experienced and eager for a challenge, jump right in. The big difference is the V-neckline that involves omitting the front stitches, which are then gradually added back on, forming the "V" shape.

experience level
Experienced

sizes
Small (Medium, Large, X-Large)

finished measurements
Bust 38 (40, 44, 48)"/91 (100, 110, 120)cm

materials
Approx total, yarn A: 468(507, 546, 624)yd/428(464, 500, 571)m chunky weight yarn

Approx total, yarn B: 165(165, 165, 220)yd/151(151, 151 201)m chunky weight yarn

Circular needles (cn): size 6 mm (10 U.S.), one 29"/73cm and two 16"/40cm, *or size to obtain gauge*

Double-pointed needles (dpn): size 6 mm (10 U.S.) *or size to obtain gauge*

4 stitch markers

Tapestry needle

gauge
12 sts = 4"/10cm in St st

Always take time to check your gauge.

This project was made with:

A: 7 (6, 7, 8) balls of Artful Yarn's (JCA) *Legend*, 83% wool/17% nylon, 1.75oz/50g = approx78 yds/71m per ball, color #1434 (robin hood)

B: 3 (3, 3, 4) balls of Reynold's *Scandal*, 40% nylon/30% wool/30% acrylic, 1.75oz/50g = approx 55yd/50m per ball, color #330 (sea-green)

instructions

collar (work B&F)

Using 29"/73cm cn and yarn A, CO 34 (35, 36, 38) sts.

K 1 row.

P 1 row.

yoke (work B&F)

Row 1 (RS): k2 left front sts, pm, k8 sleeve sts, pm, k14 (15, 16, 18) back sts, pm, k8 sleeve sts, pm, k2 right front sts.

Begin V-neck inc:

Row 1: p across, CO 1 (1 inc)—35 (36, 37, 38) sts.

Continue V-neck inc, while simultaneously beg yoke inc:

Row 2: *k to within 1 st of marker, m1, sl marker, m1, repeat from * across for each marker, k to end, CO 1 st (9 sts inc)—44 (45, 46, 47) sts.

Repeat Rows 1 and 2, 6 (7, 8, 9) times more—104 (115, 126, 137) sts.

Continue yoke inc (w/o edge inc):

Row 1 (WS): p.

Row 2 (RS): *k to within 1 st of marker, m1, sl marker, m1, repeat from * across for each marker, k to end (8 sts inc)—112 (123, 134, 145) sts.

Repeat Rows 1 and 2, 9 (10, 12, 13) times more for a total of 18 (20, 22, 24) inc rows—192 (211, 230, 249) sts.

divide yoke (work B&F)

Separate body and sleeve sts:

Row 1 (RS): k27 (30, 33, 36) left front sts, CO 1 (1, 2, 2) sts, pm, CO 1 st, place 44 (48, 52, 56) sts on 16"/40cm cn and *hold aside,* k50 (55, 60, 65) back sts, CO 1 st, pm, CO 1 (1, 2, 2) sts, place 44 (48, 52, 56) sts on 16"/40cm cn and *hold aside,* k27 (30, 33, 36) right front sts—108 (119, 132, 142) sts on main cn.

body (work B&F)

Work St st for 6 1/2 (6 1/2, 7 1/2, 7 1/2)"/16 (16, 19, 19)cm.

At beg of the next 18 rows, work St st, knitting or purling the first 2 sts tog for front edge shaping.

Cont knitting until body measures 8 1/2 (8 1/2, 9 1/2, 9 1/2)"/21 (21, 24, 24)cm from underarm to lower edge.

BO remaining sts.

sleeves (work ITR)

Using yarn A and 44 (48, 52, 56) sleeve sts on 16"/40cm cn, switch to dpn as necessary:

Join and k for 1"/2.5cm.

Beg underarm sleeve dec:

Rnd 1: k2tog, k across to last 2 sts, k2tog (2 sts dec)—42(46, 50, 54) sts.

Rnds 2–5: k.

Repeat Rnds 1 to 6, 5 (6, 7, 8) times more—32 (34, 36, 38) sts.

cuff

Using yarn B, k for 5"/13cm or until sleeve measures 12 (12 1/2, 13, 13 3/4)"/31 (32, 33, 35)cm from underarm.

BO loosely.

Work second sleeve same as the first.

body trim (work ITR)

With RS facing, using B and 29"/73cm cn:

Pick up sts along the entire edge of the cardigan, including the left and right fronts, neck edge, and bottom lower edge.

Note: You may have to use two cn needles to go all the way around.

Join and k 7 rnds.

BO loosely.

finishing

Sew body and underarms together on each sleeve.

Using tapestry needle, weave in ends.

Fold novelty yarn B edging of sweater and cuffs, in half and inward and baste in place.

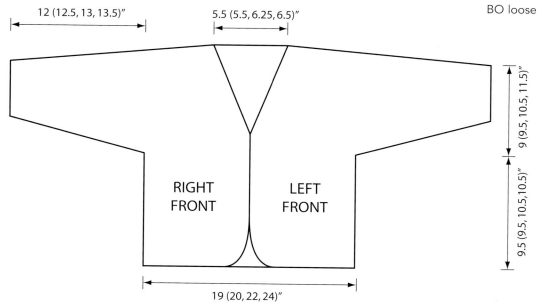

12 (12.5, 13, 13.5)"

5.5 (5.5, 6.25, 6.5)"

9 (9.5, 10.5, 11.5)"

9.5 (9.5, 10.5,10.5)"

RIGHT FRONT

LEFT FRONT

19 (20, 22, 24)"

9.5 (10, 11, 12)"

$\mathcal{P}$eony

No doubt you will look at this sweater and wonder how it is made in one piece. But follow the instructions carefully and use what you've learned so far, and it's not so hard after all! A really fun variation is to make the scarf out of one yarn type or color, and then do the body in a completely different yarn (just use a yarn of the same gauge).

experience level
Intermediate

sizes
Small (Medium, Large, X-Large)

finished measurements
Bust 36 (40, 44, 48)"/91 (102, 112, 122)cm

materials
Approx total: 840(960, 1,080, 1150)yd/768(878, 988, 1052)m heavy worsted weight yarn

Circular needles (cn): 5 mm (size 8 U.S.), one 29"/73cm, one 22"/56cm or 24"/61cm, and two 16"/40cm, *or size to obtain gauge*

Double-pointed needles: 5 mm (size 8 U.S.), 10"/26cm, *or size to obtain gauge*

4 stitch markers

Tapestry needle

Five 1/2"/1.25cm buttons

gauge
18 sts = 4"/10cm in St st

Always take time to check your gauge.

instructions

collar (work B&F)
Using 29"/73cm cn, CO 212 (224, 229, 232) sts.

Row 1: k.

Row 2: k2tog, k to end (1 st dec)—211 (223, 228, 231) sts.

Rows 3–15: repeat Row 2 (13 sts dec)—198 (210, 215, 218) sts.

Row 16: BO 63 (67, 67, 67) sts, k to end.

Row 17: repeat Row 16—63 (67, 67, 67) st dec—72 (76, 81, 84) sts.

yoke (work B&F)
Place markers:

Row 1 (RS): k15 (16, 18, 18) left front sts, pm, k9 sleeve sts, pm, k24 (26, 27, 30) back sts, pm, k9 sleeve sts, pm, k15 (16, 18, 18) right front sts, CO 4 sts (front edge)—76 (80, 85, 88) sts.

Row 2 (WS): sl 1, k3, p to end, CO 4 sts (front edge) at end—80 (84, 89, 92) sts.

Note: Keep the first 4 sts on each side in garter st, while slipping the first st of each row along the cardigan front.

Row 3 (RS): sl 1, k3, * k to 1 st of next marker, m1, sl marker, m1, repeat from

* around to each marker, k to within 2 sts to end, psso, k1, psso (buttonhole created), k1—6 sts total inc (8 sts inc; 2 buttonhole sts dec)—86 (90, 95, 98) sts.

Row 4 (WS): sl 1, k1, CO 2 sts *over the buttonhole created in the previous row,* p across, end k4—88 (92, 97, 100) sts.

Next rows: Cont in St st, keeping 4 sts at each end in garter st for front bands; at the same time, cont to alternate inc rows with purl /non-incs rows, remembering to make a buttonhole on right front side every 1 1/2"/7.5cm, for a total of 5 buttonholes (see buttonhole Row 3).

Work a total of 26 (28, 32, 35) inc rows, ending with a p row.

divide yoke (work B&F)
Separate body and sleeves:

Row 1 (RS): k41 (44, 50, 53) left front sts, CO 1 (2, 2, 2) sts, pm, CO 1 (2, 2, 2) sts, place 61 (65, 73, 79) sleeve sts on 16"/40cm cn and *hold aside,* k75 (82, 91, 100) back sts, CO 1 (2, 2, 2) sts, pm, CO 1 (2, 2, 2) sts, place 61 (65, 73, 79) sleeve sts on 16"/40cm cn and *hold aside,* k41 (44, 50, 53) right front sts—161 (178, 199, 214) sts on main cn.

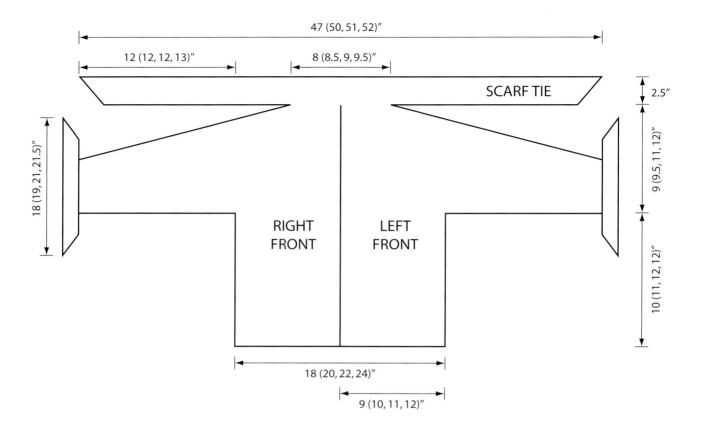

Diagram labels:
- 47 (50, 51, 52)"
- 12 (12, 12, 13)"
- 8 (8.5, 9, 9.5)"
- SCARF TIE
- 2.5"
- 18 (19, 21, 21.5)"
- 9 (9.5, 11, 12)"
- RIGHT FRONT
- LEFT FRONT
- 10 (11, 12, 12)"
- 18 (20, 22, 24)"
- 9 (10, 11, 12)"

body (work B&F)

Work St st for 9 (10, 11, 11)"/23 (25, 28, 28)cm, keeping first and last 4 sts in garter st and slipping the first st in each row.

hem

K for 1"/2.5cm.

BO loosely.

sleeves (work ITR)

Using 61 (65, 73, 79) sts on 16"/40cm cn and switching to dpn as necessary:

Rnd 1: Join and k around, CO 1 st, pm, CO 1 st at underarm (2 sts inc)—63 (67, 75, 81) sts.

K for 1"/2.5cm.

Beg underarm sleeve dec:

Rnd 1: k2tog, work around to last 2 sts, k2tog—61 (65, 73, 79) sts.

Rnds 2–5: k.

Repeat Rnds 1–5, 10 (10, 10, 11) times more—41 (45, 53, 57) sts.

cuff (work B&F)

Row 1: k sts onto 22"/56cm or 24"/61cm cn.

Row 2: CO 20 sts, k across—61 (65, 73, 77) sts.

Row 3: repeat Row 2—81 (85, 93, 97) sts.

Row 4: k2tog, k to end.

Repeat Row 4 until cuff tie measures 1"/2.5cm wide.

BO loosely.

Work second sleeve same as the first.

finishing

Sew underarms and body together on each sleeve.

Using tapestry needle, weave in ends.

Tie cuff ties into a square knot—*right over left, left over right*—so that they will lie flat, with the two ends of the ties at either side.

This project was made with:

7 (8, 9, 10) balls of Classic Elite's *Minnie*, 23% kid mohair/16% merino/38% nylon/23% polyester, 1.75oz/50g = approx 120yd/110m, #6089 (red/pink)

Cherry Blossom

This Asian-inspired top has a horizontal-patterned yoke that is split down the front. If you prefer, you can also shorten the split by joining the yoke together sooner. Both the cap sleeves and the bottom hem detail echo the mandarin collar, and they are hemmed for a smooth, finished look. This style hugs the body—fewer stitches are added at the top and, after the yoke, no stitches are added on the sides.

experience level
Intermediate

sizes
Small (Medium, Large, X-Large)

finished measurements
Bust 34 (38, 42, 46)"/86 (96, 105, 117)cm

materials
Approx total: 720(765, 810, 900)yd/659(700, 741, 823)m heavy worsted weight yarn
Circular needles (cn): 4 mm (size 6 U.S.), one 29"/73cm and two 16"/40cm, *or size to obtain gauge*
4 stitch markers
Tapestry needle
Six ¹/₂"/1.25cm pearl beads or buttons

gauge
18 sts = 4"/10cm in St st
Always take time to check your gauge.

pattern stitch
Yoke row pat (worked B&F)
Row 1 (RS): k.
Row 2: p.
Row 3: k.
Row 4: k (ridge row).

Yoke rnd pat (work ITR)
Rnd 1: k.
Rnd 2: k.
Rnd 3: k.
Rnd 4: p (ridge rnd).

instructions

collar (work B&F)

For a smooth front edge, sl 1st st in each row until the front yoke is connected:

Using 29"/73cm cn, CO 65 (70, 75, 75) sts.

Row 1: k.

Row 2: p.

Rows 3–8: rep Rows 2 and 3, 3 times more.

Row 9: p (turning ridge).

Row 10: k.

Row 11: p.

Rows 12–17: rep Rows 10 and 11, 3 times more.

Row 18: k, inc 7 (6, 6, 9) sts evenly spaced across—72 (76, 81, 84) sts.

Row 19: k.

yoke (work B&F)

Row 1 (RS): sl 1, k14 (15, 17, 17) left front sts, pm, k9 sleeve sts, pm, k24 (26, 27, 30) back sts, pm, k9 sleeve sts, pm, k15 (16, 18, 18) right front sts.

Row 2 (WS): sl 1, k1 (front band), p across, end k2.

Row 3 (RS, Inc rnd): sl 1, *k to 1 st before marker, m1, sl marker, m1*, repeat between ** across for each marker around, k to end (8 sts inc)— 80 (84, 89, 92) sts.

Row 4 (ridge row): sl 1, k to end.

Rep in order: Rows 3, 2, 3, 4, five times more.

Join and beg to work ITR:

Note: pm on right-hand needle denoting middle front.

Next row (RS): * k to 1 st before marker, m1, sl marker, m1*, repeat between ** across for each marker except middle front marker, k to end (8 sts inc)—88 (92,97,100) sts.

K 1 row.

Cont alternating an inc row with a non-inc row, while keeping to the established yoke pat, until 25 (28, 32, 35) inc rows have been completed,

ending last row at marker denoting the beg of the front sts—272 (300, 337, 364) sts.

divide yoke (work B&F)

Separate body and sleeve sts:

(RS): k80 (88, 100,106) front sts, place 59 (65, 73, 79) sleeve sts on 16"/40cm cn and *hold aside*, k74 (82, 91, 99) back sts, place 59 (65, 73, 79) sleeve sts on 16"/40cm cn and *hold aside*— 154 (170, 191, 205) sts on main cn.

body (work ITR)

K for 9 (10, 11, 12)"/22.5 (25, 27.5, 30.5) cm.

hem

Rnd 1: p.

Rnds 2–4: k.

Rnds 5–12: rep Rnds 1 to 4, 2 times more.

Rnd 13: k.

Rnd 14: p (ridge row).

Rnds 15–18: k 4 rnds.

BO loosely.

sleeves (work ITR)

Using 61 (65, 73, 79) sleeve sts on 16"/40cm cn, pm at underarm:

Rnds 1–5: k.

Rnd 6: p (ridge row).

Rnds 7–11: k.

BO loosely.

Work second sleeve same as the first.

finishing

Sew body and underarms together on each sleeve.

Using tapestry needle, weave in ends.

Fold mandarin collar inward and baste on the inside of collar. Sew buttons/beads on, each in one of the three bottom ridges and on either side of yoke (garment shown is sewn up the front until the point where the buttons begin, or you can leave it open for a more plunging neckline).

This project was made with:

8 (9, 9, 10) balls of Karabella's *Empire Silk*, 100% silk, 1.75oz/50g = approx 90yd/83m, color #508 (pink)

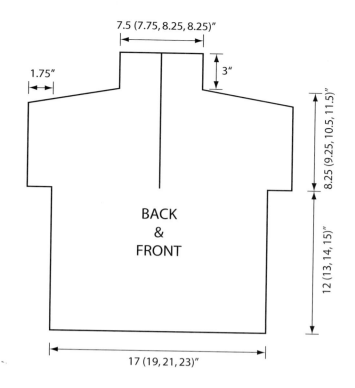

7.5 (7.75, 8.25, 8.25)"

1.75"

3"

8.25 (9.25, 10.5, 11.5)"

BACK & FRONT

12 (13, 14, 15)"

17 (19, 21, 23)"

Flame

Although a hood might seem difficult to execute, it's actually amazingly easy. A bit more daunting is incorporating the allover texture into the middle of the increases in the yoke. But, in fact, you'll find that the simplicity of the stitch itself makes it very doable. You'll be able to practice the stitch on the hood section, which is worked straight, with no shaping. Doing so will train your eyes to identify the ins and outs and layering of the stitches, in turn making the intricacies of the pattern second nature.

This project was made with:

8 (9, 10, 10) balls of Classic Elite's
Montera, 50% wool/50% llama,
3.5oz/100g = approx 127yd/116
color #3858 (cintachi red)

experience level
Intermediate

sizes
Small (Medium, Large, X-Large)

finished measurements
36 (40, 44, 48)"/91 (102, 112, 122)cm

materials
Approx total: 1016(1048, 1174, 1270)yd/(930, 959, 1074, 1162)m heavy worsted weight yarn

Circular needles (cn): 5.5 mm (size 9 U.S.), two 29"/73cm and two 16"/40cm, *or size to obtain gauge*

Double-pointed needles (dpn): 5.5 mm (size 9 U.S.), 10"/26cm, *or size to obtain gauge*

4 stitch markers

Tapestry needle

gauge
16 sts = 4"/10cm in pat st

Always take time to check your gauge.

pattern stitch
Mini-box Stitch (multiple of 4)

Row 1: * k2, p2 repeat from *.

Row 2: rep Row 1.

Row 3: * p2, k2, repeat from *.

Row 4: rep Row 3.

instructions

hood (work B&F)
Using 16"/40cm cn, CO 64 (68, 72, 76) sts.

Row 1: sl 1, k1 (front edge), * k2, p2 (pat st), repeat from * across, end k2 (front edge).

Row 2: rep Row 1.

Row 3: sl 1, k1, * p2, k2, repeat from * across, end k2.

Row 4: rep Row 3.

Next rows: rep Rows 1 to 4 until piece measures 15"/38cm.

yoke (work B&F)
Note: The top part of the yoke is knit like a cardigan—in rows, B&F. However, after 5 inc rows, you will connect the yoke and begin to work ITR to create a pullover structure. Keep the 2 sts on each side of the front in garter st until the yoke is joined.

Row 1 (RS): sl 1, k12 (13, 14, 15) left front sts, pm, k9 sleeve sts, pm, k20 (22, 24, 26) back sts, pm, k9 sleeve sts, pm, k13 (14, 15, 16) right front sts.

Row 2 (WS): sl 1, k1, p across (slip markers), end k2.

Row 3 (RS): sl 1, k1, * work pat until 1 st before marker, t1, k1, sl marker, k1, t1, repeat from * across, end k2 (8 sts inc)—72 (76, 80, 84) sts.

Row 4 (WS): sl 1, k1, work pat across purling the st before and after marker, end k2.

Rows 5–12: rep Rows 3 and 4, 4 times more.

yoke (work ITR)
Join the left and right fronts, placing a marker to denote the beg of the rnd that is now center front. The next rnd will be an inc rnd—incorporate the garter sts along the front edges into the pat.

Beginning at center front:

Rnd 1: * work pat up to 1 st of next marker, t1, k1, sl marker, k1, t1, repeat from * around for each marker, then work pat to end of rnd—center front (8 sts inc).

Rnd 2: work around in pat, keeping the 2 sts on each side of each marker in garter st.

Next rnds: rep Rnds 1 and 2, 17 (18, 23, 26) times more—248 (276, 304, 332) sts.

divide yoke (work ITR)
Separate body and sleeves:

Rnd 1 (RS): k36 (40, 44, 48) left front sts, CO 1 (1, 2, 1), pm, CO 1 (1, 2, 1), place 55 (61, 67, 73) sleeve sts on 16"/40cm cn and *hold aside*, pm, k66 (74, 82, 90) back sts, CO 1 (1, 2, 1), pm, CO 1 (1, 2, 1), place 55 (61, 67, 73) sleeve sts on 16"/40cm cn and *hold aside*, k36 (40, 44, 48) right front sts—142 (158, 168, 190) sts on main cn.

body (ITR)
Work joined front and back in pat for 8 (9, 10, 10)"/20 (23, 25, 25)cm or desired length.

Lower edge (create split hem, work back and front separately):

Beginning at center front:

Row 1: work to 2 sts before first marker, k2—*place back sts on another cn to be worked later. Using front sts only, turn:*

Row 2 (WS): k2, work pat across, end k2.

Row 3 (RS): k2, k2tog, work pat across, k2tog, k2.

Rows 4–17: rep Rows 2 and 3, 7 times more.

BO loosely in pat.

Repeat for back sts.

sleeves (work ITR)
Using 55 (61, 67, 73) sleeve sts on 16"/40cm cn, pm at underarm:

Work pat for 1"/2.5cm.

Next rnd: k2tog, work around, k2tog (2 sts dec)—53 (59, 65, 71) sts.

K 1 rnd.

Repeat last 2 rnds, 3 times more, switching to dpn as necessary—47 (53, 59, 65) sts.

Work even until sleeve measures 17 (17 1/2, 18, 18)"/43 (44, 45, 45)cm from underarm.

K 1 rnd.

P 1 rnd.

Rep last 2 rnds.

BO loosely.

Work second sleeve same as the first.

finishing

Sew body and underarms together on each sleeve.

Using tapestry needle, weave in ends.

Sew top hood seam together.

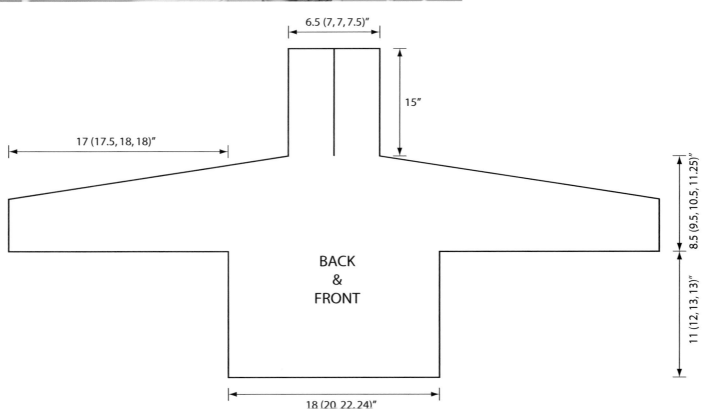

6.5 (7, 7, 7.5)"

15"

17 (17.5, 18, 18)"

8.5 (9.5, 10.5, 11.25)"

BACK
&
FRONT

11 (12, 13, 13)"

18 (20 22, 24)"

Ember

Horizontal knitted tubing, which alternates with bands of stockinette stitch and its inverse, has a simple yet elegant architecture. This particular pattern is as easy as it gets. For more fun and even more design interest, you could extend the neck upward to make a tubed turtleneck, or lengthen the sleeves, gradually making increases along the underarm to create belled tube sleeves—dramatic and fun!

experience level
Beginner

sizes
Small (Medium, Large, X-Large)

finished measurements
Bust 36 (40, 44, 48)"/91 (102, 112, 122)cm

materials
Approx total: 990(1100, 1200, 1320)yd/906(1006, 1098, 1208)m heavy worsted weight yarn

Circular needles (cn): 6 mm (size 10 U.S.), one 29"/73cm and two 16"/40cm, *or size to obtain gauge*

Double-pointed needles (dpn): 6 mm (size 10 U.S.), 10"/26cm, *or size to obtain gauge*

4 stitch markers

Tapestry needle

gauge
16 sts = 4"/10cm in St st

Always take tme to check your gauge.

instructions

collar (work ITR)
Using 16"/40cm cn, CO 60 (64, 64, 68) sts.

Rnds 1–5 (RS): p.

Rnds 6–8: k.

Rnds 9–13: p.

Rnds 14–16: k.

Rnds 17–21: p.

Rnd 22: k, inc 4 (4, 8, 8) sts evenly spaced—64 (68, 72, 76) sts.

yoke (work ITR)
Place markers:

Rnd 1 (RS): k27 (29, 31, 33) front sts, pm, k9 sleeve sts, k19 (21, 23, 25) back sts, pm, k9 sleeve sts, pm.

Rnd 2 *(Inc rnd):* m1, * k to 1 st before next marker, m1, sl marker, m1, repeat from *around, 3 times more, k around, end m1 (8 sts inc)—72 (76, 80, 84) sts.

Rnd 3: k.

Repeat Rnds 2 and 3, 22 (25, 28, 31) times more—248 (296, 304, 332) sts.

divide yoke (work ITR)
Separate body and sleeves:

Rnd 1 (RS): k73 (81, 89, 97) front sts,

CO 2 sts, pm, CO 1 st, place 55 (61, 67, 73) sleeve sts on 16"/40cm cn and *hold aside*, k65 (73, 81, 89) back sts, CO 1 st, pm, CO 2 sts, place 55 (61, 67, 73) sleeve sts on 16"/40cm cn and *hold aside*—144 (160, 176, 192) sts on main cn.

body (work ITR)

K for 1"/2.5cm.

Next rnd: * K2tog, k to 2 sts before next marker, k2tog, sl marker, repeat from * around (4 sts dec)—140 (156, 172, 188) sts.

Next rnd: K 1 rnd.

Repeat last 2 rnds twice more (8 sts dec)—132 (148, 164, 180) sts.

Note: Try the sweater on at this point to see whether the yoke length clears the bustline. You are just about to begin the patterned part and it should not bisect your bust; if it does, you might want to knit 1"/2.5cm to 2"/5cm more so that the tubing sits below the chest line.

P 2 rnds.

K 2 rnds.

P 3 rnds.

K 3 rnds.

P 4 rnds.

K 4 rnds.

P 5 rnds.

K 5 rnds.

Repeat last 10 rnds, 4 times more or to desired length.

BO loosely.

sleeves (work ITR)

Using 58 (64, 70, 76) sleeve sts on 16"/40cm cn; switch to dpn as necessary:

Join and k for 1/2"/1.3cm.

Next rnd: k2tog, k to last 2 sts, k2tog (2 st dec)—56 (62, 68, 74) sts.

K 2 rnds.

Next rnd: k2tog, k to last 2 sts, k2tog (2 st dec) —54 (60, 66, 72).

Rep last 3 rnds 5 (6, 6, 7) times more—46 (50, 54, 60) sts.

Work even, if necessary, until sleeve length is 5"/13cm from underarm.

Begin tubing:

P 5 rnds.

K 5 rnds

Repeat last 10 rnds, 4 times more.

BO loosely.

Work second sleeve same as the first.

finishing

Sew underarms and body together on each sleeve.

Using tapestry needle, weave in ends.

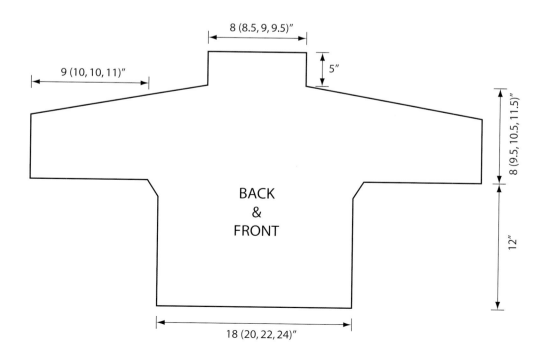

8 (8.5, 9, 9.5)"

9 (10, 10, 11)"

5"

8 (9.5, 10.5, 11.5)"

12"

BACK & FRONT

18 (20, 22, 24)"

experience level
Beginner

sizes
Small (Medium, Large, X-Large)

finished measurements
Bust 36(40, 44, 48)"/91(102, 112, 122)cm

materials
Approx total, yarn A: 988(1040, 1440, 1245)yd/904(952, 1317, 1139)m heavy worsted weight yarn

Approx total, yarn B: 208yd/190m heavy worsted weight yarn

Circular needles (cn): 6 mm (size 10 U.S.), one 29"/73cm and two 16"/40cm, *or size to obtain gauge*

Double-pointed needles (dpn): 6 mm (size 10 U.S.), 10"/26cm, *or size to obtain gauge*

4 stitch markers

Tapestry needle

gauge
16 sts = 4"/10cm in St st

Always take time to check your gauge.

note
Garter stitch done ITR is achieved by alternately knitting a round and then purling a round.

Snowberry

There are two things happening here that give this sweater a charming, vintage look: the gorgeous, soft, textured yarn and the simple, but elegant, off-set collar. The collar is achieved by making a standard polo collar—a straight, worked piece—that is overlapped at the finish. The placement of yoke markers is a slight twist that positions the collar off to the side rather than in the middle of the sweater body. It's the only unusual transition in the entire design, but it makes all the difference in the final look. For a more dramatic appearance, the collar could be extended, creating more of a swoop around the neckline.

instructions

collar (work B&F)
Using yarn B and 6 mm (size 10 U.S.) 16"/40cm cn, CO 74 (78, 82, 86) sts. K for 5"/13cm.

Form overlapping collar:

K to last 10 sts—place these last 10 sts on a dpn.

Without twisting the collar, fold one end of the cn around to meet the other, and with the dpn sts on the right-hand side, hold the dpn parallel to and in front of the sts on the needle on the left-hand side.

Using yarn B, begin to knit ITR by overlapping the collar ends (refer to page 23):

K the first st on the dpn (the st on the inside edge of the collar) together with the first st on the left-hand needle, k3 more sts in the same manner, pm, k the remainder of sts on the dpn in a similar fashion, and then k to the end of the rnd where you first placed the marker (dec 10 sts)—64 (68, 72, 76) sts.

yoke (work ITR)
Place markers:

Rnd 1: Using yarn A, k9 sleeve sts, pm, k19 (21, 23, 25) back sts, pm, k9 sleeve sts, pm, k27 (29, 31, 33) front sts, pm.

Rnd 2 (Inc rnd): m1, * k to 1 st before m1, pm, m1, repeat from * 3 times more, k around, end m1 (8 sts inc)—72 (76, 80, 84) sts.

Rnd 3: k.

Repeat Rnds 2 and 3, 22 (25, 28, 31) times more.

divide yoke (work ITR)
Separate body and sleeves:

Place 55 (61, 67, 73) sleeve sts on 16"/40cm cn and *hold aside*, CO 2 sts, pm, CO 1 st, k65 (73, 81, 89) back sts, CO 1 st, pm, CO 2 sts, place 55 (61, 67, 73) sleeve sts on 16"/40cm cn and *hold aside*, k73 (81, 89, 97) front sts—144 (160, 176, 192) sts on main cn.

body (work ITR)
K for 9 (10, 11, 11 1/2)"/23 (26, 28, 29)cm.

hem

Work garter st for 3"/7.5cm.
BO loosely.

sleeves (work ITR)

*Using 55 (61, 67, 73) sleeve sts on
16"/40cm cn:*

Rnd 1: k around, CO 1 st, pm, CO 1
st—57 (63, 69, 75) sts.

K for 1"/2.5cm.

*Underarm sleeve decs; switch to dpn
as necessary:*

Rnd 1: k2tog, k around, end k2tog (2
sts dec)—55 (61, 67, 73) sts.

Rnds 2–6: k

Repeat Rnds 1–6, 12 (13, 13, 16) times
more—31 (35, 41, 41) sts.

cuff

K for 3"/7.5cm.
BO loosely.

Work second sleeve same as the first.

finishing

Sew underarm and body together on
each sleeve.

Using tapestry needle, weave in ends.

This project was made with:

A: 10 (10, 11, 12) balls of Berroco's
Softy, 52% Dupont Tactel/48%
nylon, 1.75oz/50g = approx
104yd/95m, color #2931 (light pink)

B: 2 balls of Berroco's *Softy,* 52%
Dupont Tactel/48% nylon,
1.75oz/50g = approx 104yd/95m,
color #2939 (fuchsia)

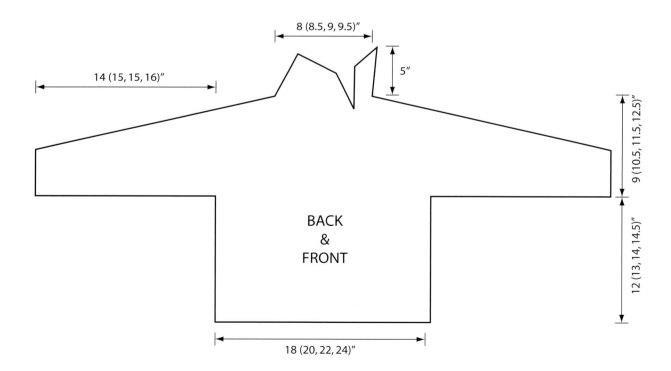

Wild Plum

Three-quarter-length sleeves, soft yarn, and a satin-ribbon tie at the waist give this rolled-collar pullover unexpected elegance. Although the yarn manufacturer recommended an 18 st/4" gauge, I found it to be closer to a 16 st/4" gauge. Given that and the extreme stretchiness of the fiber, I decided to treat it as a 16 st/4" gauge, which, when made up, isn't as baggy as one might expect. In designing, you have to decide how much drape you want in the finished sweater, keeping in mind that knits, by nature, stretch regardless. Also, remember to check gauge, even if the yarn label suggests otherwise.

experience level
Intermediate

sizes
Small (Medium, Large, X-Large)

finished measurements
Bust 36 (40, 44, 48)"/ 91(102, 112, 122) cm

materials
Approx total, yarn A: 653(671, 796, 854)yd/597(614, 728, 781)m heavy worsted weight yarn

Approx total, yarn B: 115(122, 165, 180)yd/105 (112, 151, 165)m heavy worsted weight yarn

Circular needles (cn): 4 mm (size 6 U.S.), one 29"/73cm and two 16"/40cm, or size to obtain gauge

Double-pointed needles (dpn): 4 mm (size 6 U.S.) or size to obtain gauge

4 stitch markers

Tapestry needle

2 yds ³/4"/1.9cm-wide satin ribbon

gauge
16 sts = 4"/10cm in St st

Always take time to check your gauge.

instructions

collar (work ITR)
Using 16"/40cm cn and yarn A, CO 64 (68, 72, 76) sts:

Join and k for 8 rnds.

yoke (work ITR)
Rnd 1: k27 (29, 31, 33) front sts, pm, k9 sleeve sts, pm, k19 (21, 23, 25) back sts, pm,

Rnd 2 (Inc rnd): t1, *k to next marker, t1, sl marker, k1, t1, repeat from * for each marker, k to end, t1 (8 sts inc)—72 (76, 80, 84) sts.

Rnd 3: k.

Repeat Rnds 2 and 3, 22 (25, 28, 31) times more—248 (276, 304, 332) sts.

divide yoke (work ITR)
Separate body and sleeve sts:

K73 (81, 89, 97) front sts, CO 2 sts, pm, CO 1 st, place 55 (61, 67, 73) sleeve sts on 16"/40cm cn and *hold aside*, k65 (73, 81, 89) back sts, CO 1 st, pm, CO 2 sts, place 55 (61, 67, 73) sleeve sts on 16"/40cm cn and *hold aside*—144 (160, 176, 192) sts on main cn.

body (work ITR)
K for 1"/2.5cm.

Next rnd: k2tog, k to 2 sts before next marker, k2tog, sl marker, k2tog, k to last 2 sts, k2tog (4 sts dec)—140 (156, 172, 188) sts.

Repeat Rnd 2, 3 more times—128 (144, 160, 176) sts.

K for 0 (0, 1, 2)"/0 (0, 2.5, 5)cm more or to desired length to beg of belt color.

Using yarn B (belt), k for 2"/5cm.

belt holes
Rnd 1: k7 (10, 11, 9) sts, BO next 2 sts*, repeat from * around, end k2 (0, 2, 0) sts.

Rnd 2: k and CO 2 sts over each BO space made in previous rnd.

K for 2"/5cm.

Using yarn A, k for 2"/5cm.

hem
Rnd 1 and 3: p.

Rnd 2: k.

BO loosely.

sleeves (work ITR)
Using 55 (61, 67, 73) sleeve sts on 16"/40cm cn, pm at underarm:

K for ¹/2"/1.25cm.

Underarm Shaping

Rnd 1: k2tog, k to last 2 sts, k2tog (2 sts dec)—53 (59, 65, 71) sts.

K4 (4, 4, 3) rnds.

Repeat last 5 (5, 5, 4) rnds, 9 (9, 11, 14) times more (switching to dpn as necessary)—33 (39, 41, 41) sts.

K for 9 ¹/2 (10 ¹/2, 11 ¹/2, 11 ¹/2)"/24 (27, 29, 29)cm.

cuff
Rnd 1: *k1, t1, repeat from * around—33 (39, 41, 41) inc sts—66 (78, 82, 82) sts.

K for 2"/5cm.

P 1 rnd.

BO loosely.

Work second sleeve same as the first.

finishing

Sew body and underarms together on each sleeve.

Using tapestry needle, weave in ends.

Weave ribbon through belt holes.

This project was made with:

A: 11 (11, 13, 14) balls of Muench's *Touch Me*, 72% rayon micro-fiber/28% wool, 1.75oz/50g = approx 61yd/56m per ball, color #3608 (fuchsia)

B: 2 (2, 3, 3) balls of Muench's *Touch Me*, 72% rayon micro-fiber/28% wool, 1.75oz/50g = approx 61yd/56m per ball, color #3634 (cobalt blue)

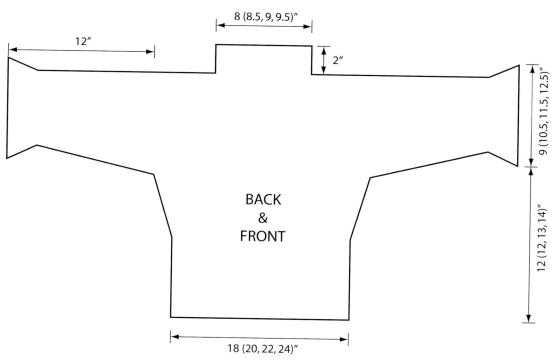

12"

8 (8.5, 9, 9.5)"

2"

9 (10.5, 11.5, 12.5)"

12 (12, 13, 14)"

BACK
&
FRONT

18 (20, 22, 24)"

Coast

Although there's a fair amount of detail in this design, it's deceptively simple to make when using the top-down technique. Like a cardigan, the sweater is split in the front and is then brought together just before the yolk ends, and is finally worked in the round to completion. This project works up quickly —start it on a Thursday and you'll have it done for the weekend.

experience level
Intermediate

sizes
Small (Medium, Large, X-Large)

finished measurements
Bust 38 (40, 44, 48)"/91 (100, 110, 120)cm

materials
Approx total: 879(925, 1110, 1180)yd/804(846, 1015, 1290)m dk weight yarn

Circular needles (cn): 4.5 mm (size 7 U.S.), two 24"/61cm or 29"/73cm and two 16"/40cm, *or size to obtain gauge*

Double-pointed needles (dpn): 4.5 mm (size 7 U.S.) *or size to obtain gauge*

4 stitch markers

Tapestry needle

1.5 yd/1.4m 6 mm lacing

gauge
20 sts = 4"/10cm in St st

Always take time to check your gauge.

instructions

collar (work B&F)
Using 16"/40cm cn, CO 80 (85, 90, 95) sts.

Work garter st for 1"/2.5cm.

Next row (RS): sl 1, k across.

Next row (WS): sl 1, k4, p across, end k5.

Repeat last 2 rows for 3 1/2"/8.75cm, ending with a WS row.

yoke (work B&F)
Place markers, slip the first st in each row as long as the yoke is being worked as a cardigan:

Row 1 (RS): sl 1, k16 (18, 19, 20) left front sts, pm, k10 sleeve sts, pm, k24 (27, 30, 33) back sts, pm, k10 sleeve sts, pm, k17 (19, 20, 21) right front sts.

Beg yoke inc:

Row 2 (WS): sl 1, k4, p across, end k5 *(keep the first and last 5 sts in garter st until the yoke is joined).*

Row 3 (RS): sl 1, * k to 1 st before marker, t1, k1, sl marker, k1, t1, repeat from * across for each marker, work to end (8 sts inc)—88 (93, 98, 103) sts.

Repeat Rows 2 and 3, until 28 (31, 35, 38) inc rows have been worked. At the same time, create eyelets for lacing holes on each side of the front band in inc rows 3, 9, 15, 21, and 26. Work these (RS) rows as follows: sl 1, k2tog, yo, k to last 5 sts, k1, k2tog, yo, k2.

divide yoke (work B&F)
Separate body and sleeves sts:

Row 1 (RS): k45 (50,55,59) left front sts, CO 2(2, 2, 3) sts, pm, CO 2 (2, 2, 3) sts, pm, place 66 (72, 80, 86) sleeve sts on 16"/40cm cn and *hold aside,* k82 (89, 100, 109) back sts, pm, place 66 (72, 80, 86) sleeve sts on 16"/40cm cn and *hold aside,* k45 (50, 55, 59) right front sts—180 (197, 218, 239) sts on main cn.

body (work ITR)

Join back and two front sides:

K for 6 (7, 8, 8)"/15 (18, 20, 20)cm, ending last row at side marker.

Beg at side marker:

Next rnd: sl marker, * p1, k to 1 st before next marker, p1, sl marker, repeat from * around once more.

K 1 rnd.

Next rnd: * P2, k to 2 sts before next marker, p2, sl marker, repeat from * around once more.

K 1 rnd.

Next rnd: * P3, k to 3 sts before next marker, p3, sl marker, repeat from * around once more.

K 1 rnd.

Next rnd: * P4, k to 4 sts before next marker, p4, sl marker, repeat from * around once more.

K 1 rnd.

Next rnd: * P5, k to 5 sts before next marker, p5, sl marker, repeat from * around once more.

Repeat last 2 rnds.

Create split hem (work B&F):

Place back sts on another 24"/61cm cn and **hold aside;** turn and begin work on front sts.

Row 1 (WS): k5, p across, end k5.

Row 2 (RS): k.

Repeat Rows 1 and 2 for 3"/7cm.

Work garter st for 1"/2.5cm.

BO loosely.

Repeat for back sts on holder.

sleeves (work ITR)

Using 66 (72, 80, 86) sleeve sts on 16"/40cm cn, pm at underarm and switch to dpn as necessary:

Rnd 1: k.

Rnd 2: k2tog, k around, end k2tog (2 sts dec)—64 (70, 78, 84) sts.

Rnd 3: p.

Rnds 4–9: repeat Rnds 2 and 3, 3 times more—58 (64, 72, 78) sts.

BO loosely.

Work second sleeve same as the first.

finishing

Sew body and underarms together on each sleeve.

Using tapestry needle, weave in ends.

Take the lacing and weave up the front as you would lace a shoe.

This project was made with:

5 (5, 6, 7) balls of Reynold's *Saucy*, 100% cotton, 3 1/2oz/100g = approx 185yd/169m, color #292 (medium blue)

3 yds/2.75m, M & J Trim's Rayon Spiral Cord, Style #00259, color (white)

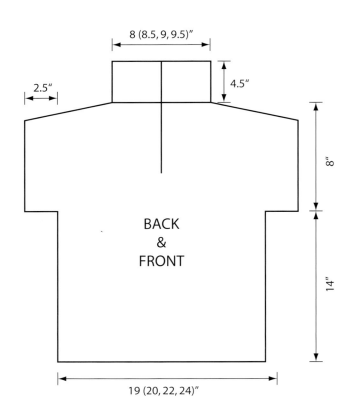

8 (8.5, 9, 9.5)"

2.5"

4.5"

8"

BACK
&
FRONT

14"

19 (20, 22, 24)"

Breeze

Beads knitted into stitches at designated intervals adorn the yoke of this versatile cardigan. In choosing beads, avoid big or heavy ones that will weigh down the yarn or even the entire sweater. Also, make sure that the bead hole is large enough to be strung on the yarn you are using. Wooden beads, such as the ones used here, are an ideal choice because they are lightweight.

experience level
Experienced

sizes
Small (Medium, Large, X-Large)

finished measurements
Bust 38 (40, 44, 48)"/92 (102, 112, 122)cm

materials
Approx total: 770(845, 924,1000)yd/702(770, 845, 915)m dk weight yarn

Circular needles (cn): 4.5 mm (size 7 U.S.), one 29"/73cm and two 16"/40cm, *or size to obtain gauge*

Crochet hook, 4.25 mm (size G/6 U.S.)

4 stitch markers

Tapestry needle

(400) 10 mm round wooden beads

gauge
20 sts = 4"/10cm in pat st

Always take time to check your gauge.

note
KB=Knit st with bead.

pattern stitch
Ridge Pattern (Work B&F)

Row 1 (WS): k (ridge row).

Row 2 (RS): k.

Row 3 (WS): p.

Row 4 (RS): k.

Ridge Pattern (Work ITR)

Rnd 1 (RS): p (ridge rnd).

Rnd 2 (RS): k.

Rnd 3 (RS): k.

Rnd 4 (RS): k.

This project was made with:

10 (11, 12, 13) balls of Classic Elite's *Bamboo*, 100% bamboo, 1 3/4oz/50g = approx 77yd/70m, color #4947 (blue)

instructions

collar (work B&F)

Using 16"/40cm cn, CO 76 (81, 86, 91) sts.

Rows 1–6: k.

Row 7: CO 2 sts, p across, CO 2 sts (4 sts inc)—80 (85, 90, 95) sts.

yoke (work B&F)

Place markers:

Row 1 (RS): sl 1, k3 (left front band), k13 (15, 16, 17) left front sts, pm, k10 sleeve sts, pm, k24 (27, 30, 33) back sts, pm, k10 sleeve sts, k13 (15, 16, 17) right front sts, k4 (right front band).

Row 2 (WS): sl 1, k3, p across, end k4.

Row 3 (RS): sl 1, k3, [* KB, k3, repeat from * across until 1 st before marker, t1, k1, sl marker, k1, t1], repeat from [ ] across for each marker, * KB, k3, repeat from * across to last 4 sts, end k4.

Row 4 (WS): sl 1, k across.

Row 5 (RS): sl 1, k3, * k to 1 st before first marker, t1, k1, sl marker, k1, t1, repeat from * across for each marker, k to end (8 sts inc)—88 (93, 98, 103) sts.

Row 6 (WS): sl 1, k3, p across, end k4.

Row 7 (RS): sl 1, k3, [k2, * KB, k3, repeat from * across until 1 st before marker, t1, k1, sl marker, k1, t1], repeat from [ ] across for each marker, k2, * KB, k3, repeat from * across to last 4 sts, end k4 (8 sts inc)—96 (101, 106, 111) sts.

Rows 8–15: rep Rows 4–6, 3 times more.

Cont in Ridge pat (see page 100), without using beads, working an inc row every other row for a total of 28 (31, 35, 38) inc rows for the yoke, ending with a WS row.

divide yoke (work B&F)

Separate body and sleeves sts:

Row 1 (RS): k45 (50, 55, 59) left front sts, CO 2 (2, 2, 3) sts, pm, CO 2 (2, 2, 3) sts, place 66 (72, 80, 86) sleeve sts on 16"/40cm cn and *hold aside*, k82 (89, 100, 109) back sts, CO 2 (2, 2, 3) sts, pm, CO 2 (2, 2, 3) sts, place 66 (72, 80, 86) sleeve sts on 16"/40cm cn and *hold*

aside, k45 (50, 55, 59) right front sts— 180 (197, 218, 239) sts on main cn.

body (work B&F)

Work in Ridge pat for 10 (11, 12, 12)"/25 (28, 30, 30)cm.

hem

Work garter st for 1"/2.5cm.

BO loosely.

sleeves (work ITR)

Using 66 (72, 80, 86) sleeve sts on 16"/40cm cn:

Next rnd: k around, CO 1 (0, 0, 1) st, pm, CO 1 (0, 0, 1) st (2 sts inc)—68 (72, 80, 88) sts.

Work 24 (28, 28, 28) rnds of Ridge pat (see note above), without beads.

cuff

Switch to dpn as necessary:

Rnd 1: * KB, k3, repeat from * around.

Rnds 2–3: k.

Rnd 4: p.

Rnd 5: k2, * KB, k3, repeat from * around.

Rnds 6–7: k.

Rnd 8: p.

Repeat Rnds 1–8, 2 times more.

Repeat Rnds 1–4 once.

Garter st edging:

K 1 rnd.

P 1 rnd.

Repeat above 2 rnds, 2 times more.

BO loosely.

Make second sleeve same as the first.

finishing

Sew body and underarms together.

Using tapestry needle, weave in ends.

tie (make 2)

Holding two strands of yarn together, make a knot, leaving a 5"/13cm tail. Using a crochet hook, chain for 9"/23cm. Thread tail with tapestry needle and then thread on 3 beads; tie at the end to secure. With the tapestry needle, attach the other end of the tie to the top front band. Make another tie and repeat.

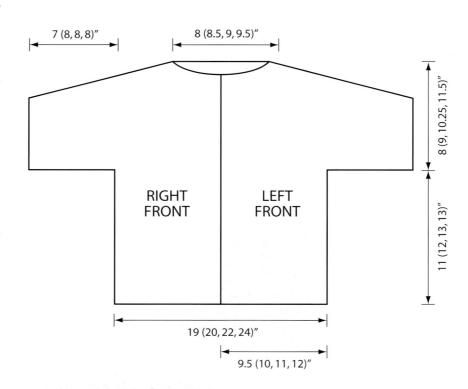

$\mathcal{B}$loom

This classic Chanel-like boxy cardigan features charming details—top-stitching on the collar and cuffs, and an energetic burst of petals on the shoulder. The metal thread shot throughout this yarn gives just the right amount of glitter (twinkly, not garish).

This project was made with:

A: 8 (9, 10, 11) balls of Rowan Classic Yarns' *Soft Lux*, 64% wool/10% angora/24% nylon/2% metallic fiber, 1.75oz/50g = 137yd/125m, color #SH004 Ciel (light blue)

B: 1 ball of Rowan Classic Yarns' *Soft Lux*, 64% wool/10% angora/24% nylon/2% metallic fiber, 1.75oz/50g = 137yd/125m, color #SH001 Pearl (white)

C: 1 ball of Rowan Classic Yarns' *Lurex Shimmer*, 80% viscose/20% polyester, 1.75oz/50g = 104yd/95m, color #SH332 (gold)

instructions

collar (work B&F)

With yarn B and 16"/40cm cn, CO 72 (77, 82, 87) sts.

Rows 1–2: k.

Work in seed st for 3 1/2"/9cm, keeping 2 sts on each side in garter st.

Change to yarn A and add front bands:

Next row: CO 4 sts (front band), work in seed st across, end CO 4 sts (front band)—80 (85, 90, 95) sts.

yoke (work B&F)

Row 1 (RS): with yarn A, sl 1, k3 (left front band), pm, k13 (15, 16, 17) left front sts, pm, k10 sleeve sts, pm, k26 (27, 30, 33) back sts, pm, k10 sleeve sts, pm, k13 (15, 16, 17) right front sts, pm, k4 (right front band).

Note: Remember to slip the first st in each row to make a smooth front edge, and keep the first 4 sts in each row in garter st for the front band.

Row 2 (WS): sl 1, k3, p across, end k4.

Row 3 (RS): sl 1, k3, * k to 1 st before marker, m1, sl marker, m1,* repeat from * across for each marker, k to end (8 sts inc)—88 (93, 98, 103) sts.

Row 4 (WS): sl 1, k3, p across, end k4.

Inc rnd with buttonhole:

Row 5 (RS): sl 1, k3, * k to 1 st before marker, m1, sl marker, m1, repeat from * across for each marker, k to within 4 sts of end, BO next 2 sts, k to end (10 sts)—94 (99, 104, 109) sts.

Row 6 (WS): sl 1, k1, CO 2 sts over buttonhole made in previous row, k1, p across, end k4—96 (101, 106, 11) sts.

Repeat Rows 3 and 4, for a total of 27 (30, 34, 37) inc rows, inserting Rows 5 and 6 for buttonhole rows every 2 (2, 2 1/2, 2 1/2)"/5 (5, 6, 6)cm, 5 times more down the front of the cardigan

past the yoke, then a final buttonhole 1"/2.5cm after 6th buttonhole or about 1/2"/1.25cm from bottom edge—304 (333, 370, 399) sts.

divide yoke (work B&F)

Separate body and sleeves sts:

Row 1 (RS): sl 1, k45 (49, 54, 58) left front sts, CO 2 (2, 2, 3) sts, pm, CO 2 (2, 2, 3) sts, place 66 (72, 80, 86) sleeve sts on 16"/40cm cn and *hold aside*, k80 (89, 100, 109) back sts, CO 2 (2, 2, 3) sts, pm, CO 2 (2, 2, 3) sts, place 66 (72, 80, 86) sleeve sts on 16"/40cm cn and *hold aside*, k46 (50, 55, 59) right front sts—180 (197, 218, 239) sts on main cn.

body (work B&F)

Work for 8 (8 1/2, 9, 9 1/2)"/20 (22, 23, 24)cm, remembering to keep 4 sts on each side in garter st and to continue to place buttonholes on right front edge (see instructions above).

hem

K 10 rows, remembering to place the last buttonhole on the right front band.

BO loosely.

sleeves (work ITR)

Using 66 (72, 80, 86) sleeve sts on 16"/40cm cn:

Next rnd: CO 1 st, pm, CO 1 st (2 sts inc)—68 (74, 82, 88) sts.

K for 1"/2.5cm.

Underarm decreases; switch to dpn as necessary:

Next rnd: K2tog, k until 2 sts from end, k2tog (2 sts dec)—66 (72, 80, 86) sts.

K 6 (6, 6, 5) rnds.

Repeat last 7 (7, 7, 6) rnds, 11 (12, 14, 17) times more—44 (46, 50, 50) sts.

experience level

Intermediate

sizes

Small (Medium, Large, X-Large)

finished measurements

Bust 36 (39, 44, 48)"/92 (99, 112, 122)cm

materials

Approx total, yarn A: 1096(1160, 1370, 1507)yd/978 (1061, 1250, 1375)m dk weight yarn

Approx total, yarn B: 100 yd/91m dk weight yarn

Approx total, yarn C: 100 yd/91m dk weight yarn

Circular knitting needles (cn): 4 mm (size 6 U.S.), one 29"/73cm and two 16"/40cm, *or size to obtain gauge*

Double-pointed needles (dpn): 4 mm (size 6 U.S.), 10"/25 m, *or size to obtain gauge*

4 stitch markers

Tapestry needle

2 yds, 3/4"/2cm-wide satin ribbon

Seven 1/2"/1.25cm buttons

gauge

20 sts = 4"/10cm in seed st

Always take time to check your gauge.

pattern stitch

Seed Stitch (multiple of 2 sts)

Row 1: * k1, p1, repeat from * across.

Row 2: * p1, k1, repeat from * across.

K until sleeve measures 14 (15, 16, 17)"/36 (38, 41, 43)cm from underarm.

cuff

Work seed st for 3"/7.6cm.

BO loosely.

Work second sleeve same as the first.

pocket (make two; work B&F)

CO 25 sts.

Work seed st for 5"/10cm.

BO.

petal (make five; work B&F)

With one strand each of yarns B and C held tog, CO 3 sts.

Row 1: p.

Row 2: k1, t1, k1, t1, k1 (2 st inc)—5 sts.

Row 3: p.

Row 4: k1, t1, k3, t1, k1 (2 sts inc)—7 sts.

Row 5: p.

Row 6: k1, t1, k5, t1, k1 (2 sts inc)—9 sts.

Row 7: p.

Row 8: k1, t1, k7, t1, k1 (2 sts inc)—11 sts.

Row 9: p.

Row 10: k.

Rows 11–18: repeat Rows 9 and 10, 4 times more.

Row 19: p.

Row 20: place 2 sts on cable needle and *hold to front*, k2tog, k2 sts from needle, k3tog, place 2 sts on cable needle and *hold to back*, k2tog, k2 sts on cable needle (4 sts dec)—7 sts.

Row 21: p2tog, p3tog, p2tog (4 sts dec)—3 sts.

Place work on dpn.

Break yarn, leaving a 10"/26cm tail.

Make 4 more petals, each time placing them on the same dpn holder with RS facing (k side of St st facing up).

With 2 strands of yarn A held tog and using the dpn with 5 petals attached (15 sts), k 2 rnds.

BO and weave in ends. Attach flower to jacket on upper shoulder with tapestry needle.

finishing

Sew body and underarms together on each sleeve.

Using tapestry needle, weave in ends.

With tapestry needle, attach completed flower to upper shoulder area.

Sew on buttons.

Finish pockets as follows:

Fold tops of pockets down about 1"/2.5cm.

Thread yarn B on a tapestry needle and make a running/basting stitch about 1/4"/6mm from the bottom of the cuffed part; place and pin the pocket to the sweater and do a running/basting stitch 1/4"/6mm from edge, around three sides of the pocket.

Finish collar as follows:

With yarn A, do a running/basting stitch about 1/4"/6mm from the edge of the collar.

Finish cuffs as follows:

Turn cuff up 1 1/2"/4cm and with yarn B, do a running/basting stitch about 1/4"/6mm from inner cuff.

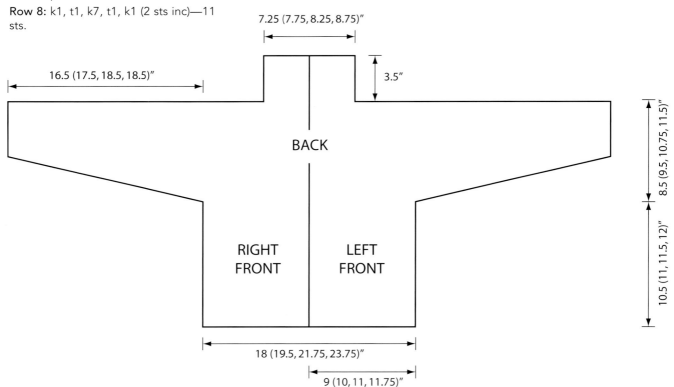

7.25 (7.75, 8.25, 8.75)"

16.5 (17.5, 18.5, 18.5)"

3.5"

BACK

RIGHT FRONT

LEFT FRONT

8.5 (9.5, 10.75, 11.5)"

10.5 (11, 11.5, 12)"

18 (19.5, 21.75, 23.75)"

9 (10, 11, 11.75)"

Stardust

Knitting with sequins is easier than ever, especially when the sequins are pre-strung into the yarn. When choosing the sequin color, make sure you coordinate the color of the string to complement the yarn. This sleeveless pullover is meant to be close fitting—if you want a looser fit, add a few increase rows (but first do the math to decide how much looser you want the top). If you want less flash—a subtler look—pick up the sequined thread only every one or two rounds instead of every round, as shown.

Intermediate

Small (Medium, Large, X-Large)

finished measurements
Bust 33 (36, 40, 43)"/84 (92, 102, 109)cm

materials
Approx total, yarn A: 737(770, 870, 960)yd/674(704, 796, 878)m dk weight yarn

Approx total, yarn B: 350(390, 420, 490)yd/320 (357,384,448)m polyester sequin thread

Circular needles (cn): 3.75 mm (size 5 U.S.), one 29"/73cm and two 16"/40cm, *or size to obtain gauge*

4 stitch markers

Tapestry needle

gauge
20 sts = 4"/10cm in seed st

Always take time to check your gauge.

pattern stitch
Seed Stitch (multiple of 2)
Row 1: * k1, p1, repeat from *.
Row 2: * p1, k1, repeat from *.

instructions

collar (work ITR)
Using 16"/40cm cn and yarn A, CO 76 (76, 80, 83) sts.

Work k1/p1 rib for 7 1/2"/19cm.

Next rnd: k, inc 4 (9, 10, 12) sts evenly spaced—80 (85, 90, 95) sts.

yoke (work ITR)
Rnd 1: k35 (38, 40, 43) front sts, pm, k10 sleeve sts, pm, k25 (27, 30, 32) back sts, pm, k10 sleeve sts, pm.

Note: Keep 1 st on each side of all 4 markers in a k st, while maintaining the seed st pat between markers.

Beg of seed st pat:
Rnd 2 (*Inc rnd*): k1, t1, * k1, p1 (seed st), until 1 st before next marker, t1, k1, sl marker, k1, t1, rep from * around for each marker, then cont in seed st until 1 st before last marker, t1, k1 (8 sts inc)—88 (93, 98, 103) sts.

Rnd 3: k1, * p the k sts and k the p sts until 1 st before marker, k1, sl marker, k1, repeat from * around for each marker, work seed st to 1 st before last marker, k1.

Repeat Rnds 2 and 3, 7 (8, 8, 9) times more—144 (157, 162, 175) sts.

divide yoke (work ITR)
Rnd 1 (*Inc rnd*): k1, t1, work front sts in seed st until 1 st before next marker, t1, k1, sl marker, p across sleeve sts, sl marker, k1, t1, work back sts in seed st until 1 st before marker, t1, k1, sl marker, p across sleeve sts (4 st inc)—148 (161, 166, 179) sts.

Cast off sleeve sts:
Rnd 2: k1, work seed st (front sts) until 1 st before marker, k1, sl marker, BO sleeve sts: k1, k2tog, BO 1 st, * k1, BO 1 st, k2tog, BO 1st, repeat from * across sleeve sts until only 1 st rem, remove marker, k2tog, k1, work seed st (back sts) until 1 st before next

marker, k1, sl marker, BO sleeve sts as before, place back sts on extra cn to be worked later.

front section (work B&F)
Using both yarn A and yarn B tog:
Row 1 (*RS, Inc row*): k2tog, k1, t1, k across until 2 sts before end, t1, k2 (2 sts inc).

Row 2 (WS): k2, p across, end k2.

Note: Keep 2 sts on each side in garter st while top front is worked.
Row 3 (*RS, Inc row*): k2, t1, k across to last 2 sts, t1, k2 (2 sts inc).

Repeat Rows 2 and 3, 17 (19, 22, 24) times more, for a total of 25 (28, 31, 34) inc rows on yoke (including the non-sequined part).

Repeat the same for back sts, starting with the inc row:
Row 1 (*RS, Inc rnd*): k2, t1, k across until 2 sts before end, t1, k2.

Row 2 (WS): k2, p across, end k2.

Repeat Rows 1 and 2, 17 (19, 22, 24) times more, for a total of 25 (28, 31, 34) inc rows on yoke (including the non-sequined part).

body (work ITR)
Using both yarn A and yarn B:
Rnd 1 (RS): k 87 (96,104, 113) front sts, pm, k 77(85, 94, 102) back sts, pm—164 (181, 198, 215) sts.

Body Shaping (skip to hem if you don't want to shape the waist—work the piece straight):

K (ITR), decreasing one st on either side of each marker (k2tog), every 1"/2.5cm, 3 times; (12 sts dec)—152(169, 186, 203) sts.

K for 10 (11, 12, 12)"/ 25 (27, 30, 30)cm.

hem

Using yarn A only, work k1/p1 rib for 2"/5cm or desired length.

BO loosely in rib.

finishing

Using tapestry needle, weave in ends.

Tip: Many of the sequins end up resting on the inside of the sweater. For an even glitzier top, use the tip of a knitting needle and gently push the sequins on the back to the front of the fabric.

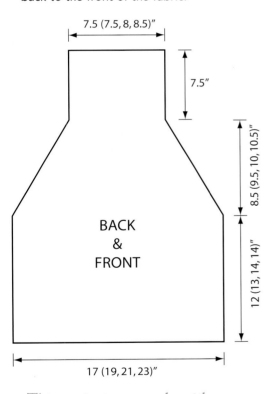

7.5 (7.5, 8, 8.5)"

7.5"

8.5 (9.5, 10, 10.5)"

BACK & FRONT

12 (13, 14, 14)"

17 (19, 21, 23)"

This project was made with:

A: 7 (7, 8, 9) balls of Blue Sky Alpacas' *Sport Weight*, 100% alpaca, 1.74oz/50g = 110yd/90m, color #308 (navy)

B: 5 (6, 6, 7) balls of Berocco's *Lazer FX*, 100% polyester, 0.35oz/10g = approx 70yd/64m, color #6004 (silver sequin/black thread)

experience level
Intermediate

sizes
Small (Medium, Large, X-Large)

finished measurements
Bust 38 (40, 43, 46)"/91 (100, 109, 117)cm

materials
Approx total, yarn A: 780(880, 930, 980)yd/713(805, 850, 896)m dk weight yarn

Approx total, yarn B: 95yd/86m dk weight yarn

Approx total, yarn C: 95yd/86m dk weight yarn

Circular knitting needles (cn): 4 mm (size 6 U.S.), one 29"/73cm and two 16"/40cm

Double-pointed needles (dpn): 4 mm (size 6 U.S.) 10"/25cm *or size to obtain gauge*

4 stitch markers

Tapestry needle

20 10mm pearls or beads

gauge
20 sts = 4"/10cm in moss st

Always take time to check gauge.

Verbena

The ruffle on this sweater is started on the outermost edge and worked inward toward the neck for full integration with the yoke. It might seem intimidating, but it's actually quite easy to do. More of a challenge (but worth the effort) is the moss stitch body. Its lovely texture provides a richness that can be easily applied to other styles.

instructions

Moss Stitch (multiple of 2)

Rnd 1: *k1, p1; rep from * around.

Rnd 2: rep Rnd 1.

Rnd 3: *p1, k1; rep from * around.

Rnd 4: rep Rnd 3.

ruffled collar (work ITR)

Beg at outer edge of ruffle with 16"/40cm cn and yarn B, CO 240 (256, 268, 282) sts.

Rnd 1: k.

Rnd 2: with yarn C, p.

Rnd 3: k.

Rnd 4: k2tog around—120 (128, 134, 141) sts.

Rnd 5: k.

Rnd 6: *k1, k2tog, rep from * around, end k 0 (2, 2, 0) sts—80 (86, 90, 94) sts.

Rnd 7: with yarn A, k.

Turn collar to WS.

Rnd 8: k.

yoke (work ITR)

Rnd 1 (RS): k35 (38, 40, 42) front sts, pm, k10 sleeve sts, pm, k25 (28, 30, 32) back sts, pm, k10 sleeve sts, pm.

Rnd 2 (*Inc rnd*): [k1, t1, * k1, p1, repeat from * until 1 sts before next marker, t1, k1, sl marker], rep from [ ] around for each marker, work moss st to end (8 sts inc)—88 (94, 98, 102) sts.

Rnd 3: k1, work moss pat (k the k sts and p the p sts), keeping 1 st each side of each marker a k st.

Rnd 4 (*Inc rnd*): [k1, t1 * p the k sts and k the p sts until 1 st before sl marker, t1, k1, sl marker], rep from [ ] around for each marker, work moss st to end (8 sts inc)—96 (102, 106, 110) sts.

Rnd 5: k1, k the k sts and p the p sts, keeping 1 st each side of each marker a k st.

Rep Rnds 2 to 5, maintaining moss st, until 29 (33, 36, 39) inc rnds are completed—312 (350, 378, 406) sts.

divide yoke (work ITR)

Rnd 1 (RS): k93 (104, 112, 120) front sts, CO 1 st so that moss st pat rem intact, place 68 (76, 82, 88) sleeve sts onto 16"/40cm cn and *hold aside*, k83 (94, 103, 110) back sts, CO 1 st so that moss st pat rem intact, place 68 (76, 82, 88) sleeve sts onto 16"/40cm cn and *hold aside*—178 (198, 216, 232) sts on main cn.

body (work ITR)

Cont to work moss st pat for 10 (11½, 12, 12½)"/25 (29, 30, 32)cm.

K 1 rnd.

P 1 rnd.

Rep last 2 rnds twice more.

BO loosely.

sleeves (work ITR)

Using 68 (76, 82, 88) sts on 16"/40cm cn, pm at underarm:

Using A, work moss st pat for 2"/5cm, making sure the pat rem intact. Note: If necessary, dec, but don't inc, 1 or 2 sts at underarm to make sure the pat works from one side to the other.

K 1 rnd.

P 1 rnd.

Rep last 2 rnds twice more.

BO loosely.

Work second sleeve same as the first.

finishing

Sew body and underarms together on each sleeve.

Weave in ends.

Sew pearls on ruffled collar: split yarn and use a third of the threads to attach individual pearls to the collar.

Sew pearls 1"/2.5cm apart around collar between ruffles.

This project was made with:

A: 8 (9, 10, 10) balls of Karabella's *Zodiac,* 100% cotton, 1.75oz/50g = approx 98yd/90m, color #476 (perwinkle)

B: 1 ball of Karabella's *Zodiac,* 100% cotton, 1.75oz/50g = approx 98yd/90m, color #411 (yellow)

C: 1 ball of Karabella's *Zodiac,* 100% cotton, 1.75oz/50g = approx 98yd/90m, color #407 (pink)

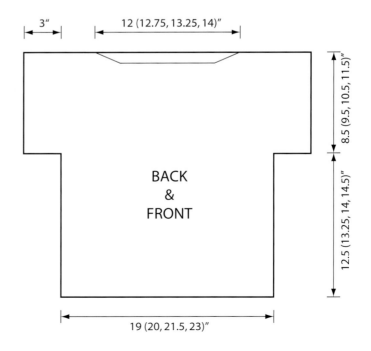

3"

12 (12.75, 13.25, 14)"

8.5 (9.5, 10.5, 11.5)"

BACK
&
FRONT

12.5 (13.25, 14, 14.5)"

19 (20, 21.5, 23)"

Violet

Stripes are easy to make, but seldom flattering. In this design, they're made wide for boldness, but are tempered by an array of tonal colors. Perhaps most importantly, the shape of the sweater itself has been streamlined with ribbing on the body sides and underarms, taking in what would otherwise be floppy extra material. You can make the sweater even more form-fitting by extending the ribbing, or you could even rib the entire sweater for the ultimate in body-hugging fit.

experience level
Intermediate

sizes
Small (Medium, Large, X-Large)

finished measurements
Bust 36 (40, 44, 48)"/91 (100, 110, 120)cm

materials
Three colors (A), (B), (C) for an approx total: 1237 (1350, 1575, 1685)yd/1132 (1912, 1440, 1541)m dk weight yarn

Circular needles (cn): size 4 mm (6 U.S.), one 29"/73cm, two 16"/40cm *or size to obtain gauge*

Double-pointed needles (dpn): size 4 mm (6 U.S.), 10"/24cm

4 stitch markers

Tapestry needle

gauge
20 sts = 4"/10cm in St st

Always take time to check gauge.

This project was made with:

instructions

collar (work ITR)

Using 16"/40cm cn and yarn B, CO 80 (84, 88, 92) sts:

Join and rib k2/p2 for 1¹/2"/2cm, inc 0 (1, 2, 3) sts evenly spaced on last rnd—80 (85, 90, 95) sts.

yoke (work ITR)

Place markers:

Rnd 1 (RS): using yarn C, k35 (38, 40, 43) front sts, pm, k10 sleeve sts, pm, k25 (27, 30, 32) back sts, pm, k10 sleeve sts, pm.

Rnd 2 *(Inc rnd)*: m1, * k to 1 st before next marker, m1, pm, m1, repeat * for each marker around, k until 1 st remains, m1 (8 sts inc)—88 (93, 98, 103) sts.

Repeat Rnds 1 and 2, 27 (30, 34, 37) times more, changing yarn colors every 21st row, in the following color order after color C: A, B, C, A, B—304 (333, 370, 399) sts.

divide yoke (work ITR)

Separate body and sleeves sts:

Rnd 1: K91 (100, 110, 119) front sts, CO 2 (2,2,3) sts, pm CO 2 (2,2,3) sts, place 66 (72, 80, 86) sts on 16"/40cm cn and *hold aside*, k81 (89, 100, 108)

back sts, CO 2 (2,2,3) sts, pm CO 2(2,2,3) sts, place 66 (72, 80, 86) sleeve sts on 16"/40cm cn and *hold aside*—180 (197, 218, 239) sts on main cn.

body (work ITR)

Using sts on main cn and keeping in stripe pat:

K for ¹/2"/1.25cm.

Next rnd: [*K2, p2, repeat from * around 4 (4, 6, 6) times, k to 18 (18, 26, 26) sts before second side marker, *p2, k2, repeat from * to end] repeat from [ ] one more time.

Cont ribbing on the sides (k the k sts, p the p sts), changing colors every 21st row, 3 (3, 4, 4) times, making 4 (4, 5, 5) stripes or desired length.

hem

Using yarn C, work in 1 rnd in est pat.

Keeping rib k2/p2 at sides, cont to k2/p2 rib across the entire front and back—inc or dec the least amount of sts necessary (1-2 sts) to match the ribbing pat on the sides.

Work 20 rnds in est rib.

BO loosely.

sleeves (work ITR)

Using 66 (72, 80, 86) sleeve sts on 16"/40cm cn:

Next rnd: k around, CO 1 st, pm, CO 1 st at underarm.

K for 1"/ 2.5cm

Insert underarm ribbing, switching to dpn as necessary:

*K2, p2, repeat from * around, 3 (3, 5, 5) times more, k to 14 (14, 22, 22) sts before marker, *p2, k2, repeat from * to end. Keep in established pat (k the k st and p the p sts), changing colors every 21st row, 4 (4, 5, 5) times as follows: A, B, C, A, B, making 5 (5, 6, 6) stripes.

cuff

Using yarn B and keeping to est k2/p2 rib pat at underarm, cont to rib across the St st area. Inc or dec the minimum sts necessary to match the pat at the other side.

Work in est pat for 2"/5cm.

BO loosely in rib.

finishing

Sew body and underarms together on each sleeve.

Using tapestry needle, weave in ends.

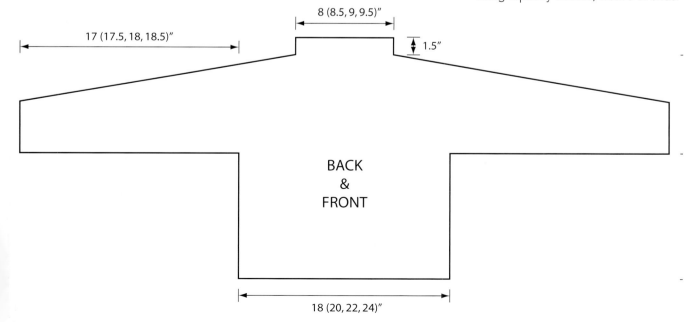

8 (8.5, 9, 9.5)"

17 (17.5, 18, 18.5)"

1.5"

BACK
&
FRONT

18 (20, 22, 24)"

asic Patterns

Basic patterns are templates from which to create your own sweaters. They are general instructions, not complete patterns, for pullover and cardigan shapes in various gauges. Stitch counts outline the basic sweater shape. Use the design ideas at the front of the book to decide what type of collar and cuffs to add, as well as how to form the body and shape the sleeves.

Note: The cardigan template does not include stitches for front bands—the instructions are for an open-front cardigan. If you want to include front bands for buttonholes, to create an overlap, add "1-inch worth" of sts on both sides; so for example, for 2 to 2 1/2 sts/in gauge add 2 sts to each side, for 3 to 3 1/2 sts/in gauge, add 3 sts, etc.

basic bulky pullover: 8 st gauge

sizes
Small (Medium, Large, X-Large)

finished measurements
Bust 32–34 (36-38, 40-42, 44-46)"/81–86 (92–97, 102–107, 112–117)cm

Garment 36 (40, 44, 48)"/91 (102, 112, 122)cm

materials
Yarn: 500 (600, 650, 750) yd /457 (549, 595, 686)m bulky weight yarn

Needles: 9-10 mm (size 13-15 U.S.) *or size to obtain gauge*

Circular (cn): one 29"/74cm, two 16"/40cm *or size to obtain gauge*

Double-pointed (dpn): 10"/25cm set

Tapestry needle

gauge
8 sts/10 rows = 4"/10cm in
Always take time to check your gauge.

instructions

collar (work ITR)
Using 16"/40cm cn, CO 32 (34, 36, 38) sts. Work collar.

yoke (work ITR)
Place markers:
Rnd 1 (RS): k13 (14, 15, 16) front sts, pm, k5 sleeve sts, pm, k9 (10, 11, 12) back sts, pm, k5 sleeve sts, pm.

Rnd 2 (*Inc rnd*): m1, *k to 1 st before marker, m1, sl m, m1, repeat from * around 3 times more, k until 1 st remains, m1 (8 sts inc)—40 (42, 44, 46) sts.

Rnd 3: k (sl markers along the way).

Repeat Rnds 2 and 3, 11 (12, 13, 15) times more—128 (138, 148, 166) sts.

basic bulky pullover: 10 st gauge

divide yoke (work ITR)

Separate body and sleeve sts:

RS: k37 (40, 43, 48) front sts, CO 1 (1, 2, 1) sts, pm, CO 0 (1, 1, 1) st, place 29 (31, 33, 37) sleeve sts on 16"/40cm cn and *hold aside*, k33 (36, 39, 44) back sts, CO 0 (1, 1, 1) st, pm, CO 1 (1, 2, 1) st, place 29 (31, 33, 37) sleeve sts on 16"/40cm cn and *hold aside*—72 (80, 88, 96) body sts remain on main cn.

body (work ITR)

Join front and back portions, work for 11 (12, 13, 14)"/28 (31, 33, 36)cm or to desired length.

hem

Work for 2"/5cm.

BO loosely.

sleeves (work ITR; wrist-length and tapered)

Work each sleeve separately, changing to dpn as necessary:

Using 29 (31, 33, 37) sts on 16"/40cm cn, CO 1 st, pm (underarm), CO 1 st—31 (33, 35, 39) sts.

Work for 1"/2.5cm.

Beg underarm sleeve dec:

Next rnd: k2tog, work around, end k2tog (2 st dec)—29 (31, 33, 37) sts.

Work 4 (5, 4, 3) rnds, repeat last 5 (6, 5, 4) rnds, 6 (1, 5, 8) times more.

Next rnd: k2tog, work around, end k2tog (2 st dec).

Work 0 (4, 3, 2) rnds, repeat last 0 (5, 4, 3) rnds, 0 (4, 1, 0) times more—17 (19, 19, 19) sts.

cuff

Work for 2"/5cm.

BO loosely.

Work second sleeve same as the first.

finishing

Sew underarms together and weave in ends.

---

sizes

Small (Medium, Large, X-Large)

finished measurements

Bust: 32–34 (36-38, 40-42, 44-46)"/81–86 (92-97, 102-107, 112-117)cm

Garment 36 (40, 44, 48)"/91 (102, 112, 122)cm

materials

Yarn: 625 (675, 750, 800)yd/572(618, 686, 732)m bulky weight yarn

Needles: 9-10 mm (size 13-15 U.S.) or size to obtain gauge

Circular (cn): one 29"/74cm, two 16"/40cm,

Double-pointed (dpn): 10"/25cm set

4 stitch markers

Tapestry needle

gauge

10 sts/12 rows = 4"/10cm

Always take time to check your gauge.

instructions

collar (work ITR)

Using 16"/40cm cn, CO 40 (42, 45, 48) sts.

Work collar.

yoke (work ITR)

Place markers:

Rnd 1 (RS): k16 (17, 19, 20) front sts, pm, k6 sleeve sts, pm, k12 (13, 14, 16) back sts, pm, k6 sleeve sts, pm.

Rnd 2 *(Inc rnd)*: m1, *k to 1 st before marker, m1, sl m, m1, repeat from * around 3 times more, k until 1 st remains, m1 (8 sts inc)—48 (50, 52, 56) sts.

Rnd 3: k (sl markers along the way).

Repeat Rnds 2 and 3, 13 (15, 17, 19) times more—152 (170, 189, 208) sts.

---

divide yoke (work ITR)

Separate body and sleeve sts:

RS: k44 (49, 55, 60) front sts, CO 2 (2, 1, 1) sts, pm, CO 1 st, place 34 (38, 42, 46) sleeve sts on 16"/40cm cn and *hold aside*—k40 (45, 50, 56) back sts, CO 1 st, pm, CO 2 (2, 1, 1) sts, place 34 (38, 42,46) sleeve sts on 16"/40cm cn and *hold aside*—90 (100, 109, 120) body sts remain on main cn.

body (work ITR)

Join front and back portions and work for 11 (12, 13, 14)"/28 (31, 33, 36)cm or desired length.

hem

Work for 2"/5cm.

BO loosely.

sleeves (work ITR; wrist-length and tapered)

Work each sleeve separately, changing to dpn as necessary:

Using 34 (38, 42, 46) sts on 16"/40cm cn, cn, CO 1 st, pm (underarm) CO 1 st—36 (40, 44, 48) sts.

Work for 1"/2.5cm.

Beg underarm sleeve dec:

Next rnd: k2tog, work around, end k2tog (2 st dec)—34 (38, 42, 46).

Work 5 (4, 4, 4) rnds, repeat last 6 (5, 5, 5) rnds, 1 (7, 8, 2) times more.

K2tog, work around, end k2tog (2 st dec).

Work 4 (3, 0, 3) rnds, repeat last 5 (4, 0, 4) rnds, 5 (0, 0, 7) times more—20 (22, 26, 26) sts.

cuff

Work for 2"/5cm.

BO loosely.

Work second sleeve same as the first.

finishing

Sew underarms together and weave in ends.

basic bulky cardigan: 8 st gauge

size
Small (Medium, Large, X-Large)

finished measurements
Bust 32–34(36-38, 40-42, 44-46)"/81–86 (92–97, 102–107, 112–117)cm

Garment 36(40, 44, 48)"/91(102, 112, 122)cm

materials
Yarn: 500 (600, 650, 750)yd /457 (549, 595, 686)m bulky weight yarn

Needles: 9-10 mm (size 13-15 U.S.) or size to obtain gauge

Circular (cn): one 29"/74cm, two 16"/41cm or size to obtain gauge

Double-pointed (dpn): 10"/ 25cm

4 stitch markers

Tapestry needle

gauge
8 sts/10 rows = 4"/10cm

Always take time to check your gauge.

instructions

collar (work B&F)
Using 16"/40cm cn, CO 32 (34, 36, 38) sts.
Work collar.

yoke (work B&F)
Place markers:
Row 1 (RS): k7 (7, 8, 8) left front sts, pm, k5 sleeve sts, pm, k8 (10, 10, 12) back sts, pm, k5 sleeve sts, pm, k7 (7, 8, 8) left front sts.

Row 2 (WS): p (slip markers along the way).

Row 3 (*Inc row*): *k to 1 st before next marker, m1, sl m, m1, repeat from * across 3 times more, k to end—40 (42, 44, 46) sts.

Repeat Rows 2 and 3, 11 (12, 13, 15) times more—128 (138, 148,166) sts.

divide yoke (work B&F)
Separate body and sleeve sts:
RS: k19 (20, 22, 24) left front sts, CO 1 (1, 2, 1) sts, pm, CO 0 (1, 1, 1) sts, place 29 (31, 33, 37) sleeve sts on 16"/40cm cn and *hold aside,* k32 (36, 38, 44) back sts, CO 0 (1, 1, 1) st, pm, CO 1 (1, 2, 1) sts, place 29 (31, 33, 37) sleeve sts on 16"/40cm cn and *hold aside,* k19 (20, 22, 24) right front sts—72 (80, 88, 96) body sts remain on main cn.

body (work B&F)
Join front and back portions and work for 11 (12, 13, 14)"/28 (31, 33, 36)cm or desired length.

hem
Work for 2"/5cm.
BO loosely.

sleeves (work ITR; wrist length and tapered)
Work each sleeve separately, changing to dpn as necessary:
Using 29 (31, 33, 37) sts on 16"/40cm cn, CO 1 sts, pm (underarm) CO 1 st—31 (33, 35, 39) sts.

Work for 1"/2.5cm.

Beg underarm sleeve dec:
Next rnd: k2tog, work around, end k2tog (2 st dec)—29(31, 33, 37) sts.

Work 4 (5, 4, 3) rnds, repeat last 5 (6, 5, 4) rnds, 6 (1, 5, 8) times more.

Next rnd: k2tog, work around, end k2tog (2 st dec).

Work 0 (4, 3, 2) rnds, repeat last 0 (5, 4, 3) rnds 0 (4, 1, 0) times more—17 (19, 19, 19) sts.

cuff
Work for 2"/5cm.
BO loosely.

Work second sleeve same as the first.

finishing
Sew underarms together and weave in ends.

basic bulky cardigan: 10 st gauge

size
Small (Medium, Large, X-Large)

finished measurements
Bust 32–34 (36-38, 40-42, 44-46)"/81–86 (92-97, 102-107, 112-117)cm

Garment 36 (40, 44, 48)"/91 (102, 112, 122)cm

materials
Yarn: 625 (675, 750, 800)yd /572(618, 686, 732)m bulky weight yarn

Needles: 9-10 mm (size 13-15 U.S.) or size to obtain gauge

Circular (cn): one 29"/74cm, two 16"/41cm or size to obtain gauge

Double-pointed (dpn): 10"/25cm set

4 stitch markers

Tapestry needle

gauge
10 sts/12 rows = 4"/10cm

Always take time to check your gauge.

instructions

collar (work B&F)
Using 16"/40cm cn, CO 40 (42, 45, 48) sts.
Work collar.

yoke (work B&F)
Row 1 (RS): k8 (9, 10, 10) left front sts, pm, k6 sleeve sts, pm, k12 (12, 13, 16) back sts, pm, k6 sleeve sts, pm, k8 (9, 10, 10) left front sts.

Row 2 (WS): p (sl markers along the way).

Row 3 (*Inc row*): *k to 1 st before next marker, m1, sl m, m1, repeat from * across 3 times more, k to end—48 (50, 52, 56) sts.

Repeat Rows 2 and 3, 13 (15, 17, 19) times more—152 (170, 189, 208) sts.

divide yoke (work B&F)

Separate body and sleeve sts:
RS: k22 (25, 28, 30) left front sts, CO 2 (2, 1, 1) sts, pm, CO 1 st, place 34 (38, 42, 46) sleeve sts on 16"/40cm cn and *hold aside,* k40 (44, 49, 56) back sts, CO 0 (0, 1, 1) st, pm, CO 0 (0, 1, 1) st, place 34 (38, 42, 46) sleeve sts on 16"/40cm cn and *hold aside,* k22 (25, 28, 30) right front sts—90 (100, 109, 120) body sts remain on main cn.

body (work B&F)

Join front and back portions, work for 11 (12, 13, 14)"/28 (31, 33, 36)cm or desired length.

hem

Work for 2"/5cm.

BO loosely.

sleeves (work ITR)

Work each sleeve separately, changing to dpn as necessary:
Using 34 (38, 42, 46) sts on 16"/40cm cn, CO 1 st, pm (underarm) CO 1 st—36 (40, 44, 48) sts.

Work for 1"/2.5cm.

Beg underarm sleeve dec:
Next rnd: k2tog, work around, end k2tog (2 st dec)—34 (38, 42, 46) sts.

Work 5 (4, 4, 4) rnds, repeat last 6 (5, 5, 5) rnds, 1 (7, 8, 2) times more.

Next rnd: k2tog, work around, end k2tog (2 st dec).

Work 4 (3, 0, 3) rnds, repeat last 5 (4, 0, 4) rnds, 5 (0, 0, 7) times more—20 (22, 26, 26) sts.

cuff

Work for 2"/5cm.

BO loosely.

Work second sleeve same as the first.

finishing

Sew underarms together and weave in ends.

---

sizes

Small (Medium, Large, X-Large)

finished measurements

Bust 32–34 (36-38, 40-42, 44-46)"/81–86(92–97, 102–107, 112–117)cm

Garment 36 (40, 44, 48)"/91 (102, 112, 122)cm

materials

Yarn: 700 (775, 875, 950) yd/640 (709, 800, 869) m chunky weight yarn

Needles: 6-6.5 mm (10-11 US) or size *to obtain gauge*

Circular (cn): one 29"/74cm, two 16"/40cm *or size to obtain gauge*

Double-pointed (dpn): 10"/25cm set

4 stitch markers

Tapestry needle

gauge

12 sts/16 rows = 4"/10cm
Always take time to check your gauge.

instructions

collar (work ITR)

Using 16"/40cm cn, CO 48 (51, 54, 57) sts.
Work collar.

yoke (work ITR)

Place markers:
Rnd 1 (RS): k19 (21, 22, 24) front sts, pm, k8 sleeve sts, pm, k13 (14, 16, 17) back sts, pm, k8 sleeve sts, pm.

Rnd 2 *(Inc row):* m1, *k to 1 st before marker, m1, sl m, m1, repeat from * around 3 times more, k until 1 st remains, m1 (8 sts inc)—56 (59, 62, 65) sts.

Rnd 3: k (sl markers along the way).

Repeat Rnds 2 and 3, 17 (19, 21, 23) times more—192 (211, 230, 249) sts.

---

divide yoke (work ITR)

Separate body and sleeve sts:
RS: k55 (61, 66, 72) front sts, CO 1 (1, 2, 2) sts, pm, CO 1 st, place 44 (48, 52, 56) sleeve sts on 16"/40cm cn and *hold aside,* k49 (54, 60, 65) back sts, CO 1 st, pm, CO 1 (1, 2, 2) sts, place 44 (48, 52, 56) sleeve sts on 16"/40cm cn and *hold aside*—108 (119, 132, 143) body sts remain on main cn.

body (work ITR)

Join front and back portions, work for 11 (12, 13, 14)"/28 (31, 33, 36)cm.

hem

Work for 2"/5cm.

BO loosely.

sleeves (work ITR; wrist-length and tapered)

Work sleeves separately, changing to dpn as necessary:
Using 44 (48, 52, 56) sts on 16"/40cm cn, CO 1 st, pm (underarm), CO 1 st. 46 (50, 54, 58) sts.

Work for 1"/2.5cm.

Beg underarm sleeve dec:
Next rnd: k2tog, work around, end k2tog (2 sts dec)—44 (48, 52, 56) sts.

Work 4 (5, 4, 4) rnds, repeat last 5 (6, 5, 5) rnds, 10 (2, 11, 5) times more.

Next rnd: k2tog, work around, end k2tog (2 sts dec).

Work 0 (4, 0, 3) rnds, repeat last 0 (5, 0, 4) rnds, 0 (7, 0, 7) times more—24 (28, 30, 30) sts.

cuff

Work for 2"/5cm.

BO loosely

Work second sleeve same as the first.

finishing

Sew underarms together and weave in ends.

basic chunky pullover: 10 st gauge

sizes
Small (Medium, Large, X-Large)

finished measurements
Bust 32–34 (36-38, 40-42, 44-46)"/81–86 (92–97, 102–107, 112–117)cm

Garment: 36 (40, 44, 48)"/91 (102, 112, 122)cm

materials
Yarn: 775 (900, 1100, 1250) yd/709 (823, 1006, 1144)m chunky weight yarn

Needles: 6-6.5 mm (10-11 US) *or size to obtain gauge*

Circular (cn): one 29"/74cm, two 16"/40cm *or size to obtain gauge*

Double-pointed (dpn): 10"/25cm set

4 stitch markers

Tapestry needle

gauge
14 sts/18 rows = 4"/10cm

Always take time to check your gauge.

instructions

collar (work ITR)
Using 16"/40cm cn, CO 56 (59, 63, 66) sts.

Work collar.

yoke (work ITR)
Place markers:

Rnd 1 (RS): k23 (25, 27, 28) front sts, pm, k8 sleeve sts, pm, k17 (18, 20, 20) back sts, pm, k8 sleeve sts, pm.

Rnd 2 *(Inc row):* m1, *k to 1 st before marker, m1, sl m, m1, repeat from * around 3 times more, k until 1 st remains, m1 (8 sts inc)—64 (67, 71, 74) sts.

Rnd 3: k (sl markers along the way).

Repeat Rnds 2 and 3, 19 (22, 25, 27) times more—216 (243, 271, 290) sts.

divide yoke (work ITR)
Separate body and sleeve sts:

RS: k63 (71, 79, 84) front sts, CO 1 (1, 1, 2) sts, pm, CO 1 st, place 48 (54, 60, 64) sleeve sts on 16"/40cm cn and *hold aside*, k57 (64, 72, 78) back sts, CO 1 st, pm, CO 1 (1, 1, 2) sts, place 48 (54, 60, 64) sleeve sts on 16"/40cm cn and *hold aside*—124 (139, 155, 168) body sts remain on main cn.

body (work ITR)
Join front and back portions, work body for 11 (12, 13, 14)"/28 (31, 33, 36)cm.

hem
Work for 2"/5cm.

BO loosely.

sleeves (work ITR)
Work sleeves separately, changing to dpn as necessary:

Using 48 (54, 60, 64) sts on 16"/40cm cn, CO 1 st, pm (underarm), CO 1 st—50 (56, 62, 66) sts.

Work for 1"/2.5cm.

Beg underarm sleeve dec:

Next rnd: k2tog, work around, end k2tog (2 sts dec)—48 (54, 60, 64) sts.

Work 5 (5, 4, 4) rnds, repeat last 6 (6, 5, 5) rnds, 7 (5, 11, 5) times more.

Next rnd: k2tog, work around, end k2tog (2 sts dec).

Work 4 (4, 3, 3) rnds, repeat last 5 (5, 4, 4) rnds, 2 (5, 1, 9) times more—28 (32, 34, 34) sts.

cuff
Work for 2"/5cm.

BO loosely.

Work second sleeve same as the first.

finishing
Sew underarms together and weave in ends.

basic chunky cardigan: 8 st gauge

sizes
Small (Medium, Large, X-Large)

finished measurements
Bust 32–34 (36-38, 40-42, 44-46)"/81–86(92–97, 102–107, 112–117)cm

Garment 36 (40, 44, 48)"/91 (102, 112, 122)cm

materials
Yarn: 700 (775, 875, 950) yd/640 (709, 800, 869)m chunky weight yarn

Needles: 6-6.5 mm (10-11 US) *or size to obtain gauge*

Circular (cn): one 29"/74cm, two 16"/40cm or

Double-pointed (dpn): 10"/25cm set

4 stitch markers

Tapestry needle

gauge
12 sts/16 rows = 4"/10cm

Always take time to check your gauge.

instructions

collar (work B&F)
Using 16"/40cm cn, CO 48 (51, 54, 57) sts.

Work collar.

yoke (work B&F)
Place markers:

Row 1 (RS): k9 (10, 11, 12) left front sts, pm, k8 sleeve sts, pm, k14 (15, 16, 17) back sts, pm, k8 sleeve sts, pm, k9 (10, 11, 12) right front sts.

Row 2 (WS): p (sl markers along the way).

Row 3 *(Inc row):* *k to 1 st before next marker, m1, sl m, m1, repeat from * across 3 times more, k to end—56 (59, 62, 65) sts.

Repeat Rows 2 and 3, 17 (19, 21, 23) times more—192 (211, 230, 249) sts.

divide yoke (work B&F)
Separate body and sleeve sts:
RS: k27 (30, 33, 36) left front sts, CO 1 (1, 2, 2) sts, pm, CO 1 sts, place 44 (48, 52, 56) sleeve sts on 16"/40cm cn and *hold aside*, k50 (55, 60, 65) back sts, CO 1 st, pm, CO 1 (1, 2, 2) st, place 44 (48, 52, 56) sleeve sts on 16"/40cm cn and *hold aside*—108 (119, 132, 143) body sts remain on main cn.

body (work B&F)
Join front and back portions, work for 11 (12, 13, 14)"/28 (31, 33, 36)cm.

hem
Work for 2"/5cm.

BO loosely.

sleeves (work ITR)
Work sleeves separately, changing to dpn as necessary:
Using 44 (48, 52, 56) sts on16"/40cm cn,

CO 1 st, pm (underarm), CO 1 st—46 (50, 54, 58) sts.

Work for 1"/2.5cm.

Beg underarm sleeve dec:
Next rnd: k2tog, work around, end k2tog (2 st dec)—44 (48, 52, 56) sts.

Work 4 (5, 4, 4) rnds, repeat last 5 (6, 5, 5) rnds, 10 (2, 11, 5) times more.

Next rnd: k2tog, work around, end k2tog (2 st dec).

Work 0 (4, 0, 3) rnds, repeat last 0 (5, 0, 4) rnds, 0 (7, 0, 7) times more—24 (28, 30, 30) sts.

cuff
Work for 2"/5cm.

BO loosely.

Work second sleeve same as the first.

finishing
Sew underarms together and weave in ends.

---

basic chunky cardigan: 10 st gauge

sizes
Small (Medium, Large, X-Large)

finished measurements
Bust 32–34 (36-38, 40-42, 44-46)"/81–86(92–97, 102–107, 112–117)cm

Garment 36 (40, 44, 48)"/91 (102, 112, 122)cm

materials
Approx total: 775(900, 1100, 1250 yd/709 (823, 1006, 1144)m chunky weight yarn

Needles: 6-6.5 mm (10-11 US) *or size to obtain gauge*

Circular (cn): one 29"/74cm, two 16"/40cm *or size to obtain gauge*

Double-pointed (dpn): 10"/25cm set

4 stitch markers

Tapestry needle

gauge
14 sts/18 rows = 4"/10cm
Always take time to check your gauge.

instructions
collar (work B&F)
Using 16"/40cm cn, CO 56 (59, 63, 66) sts.
Work collar.

yoke (work B&F)
Row 1 (RS): k11 (12, 13, 14) left front sts, pm, k8 sleeve sts, pm, k18 (19, 21, 22) back sts, pm, k8 sleeve sts, pm, k11 (12, 13, 14) right front sts.

Row 2 (WS): p (sl markers along the way).

Row 3 *(Inc row):* *k to 1 st before next marker, m1, sl m, m1, repeat from * across 3 times more, k to end—64 (67, 71, 74) sts.

Repeat Rows 2 and 3, 19 (22, 25, 27) times more—216 (243, 271, 290) sts.

---

divide yoke (work B&F)
Separate body and sleeve sts:
RS: k31 (35, 39, 42) front sts, CO 1 (1, 1, 2) sts, pm, CO 1 st, place 48 (54, 60, 64) sleeve sts on 16"/40cm cn and *hold aside*, k58 (65, 73, 78) back sts, CO 1 st, pm, CO 1 (1, 1, 2) sts, place 31 (35, 39, 42) sleeve sts on 16"/40cm cn and *hold aside*— 124 (139, 155, 168) body sts remain on main cn.

body (work B&F)
Join front and back portions, work for 11 (12, 13, 14)"/28 (31, 33, 36)cm.

hem
Work for 2"/5cm.

BO loosely.

sleeves (work ITR; wrist-length and tapered)
Work sleeves separately, changing to dpn as necessary:
Using 48 (54, 60, 64) sts on 16"/40cm cn,

CO 1 at, pm (underarm), CO 1 st—50 (56, 62, 66) sts.

Work for 1"/2.5cm.

Beg underarm sleeve dec:
Next rnd: k2tog, work around, end k2tog (2 st dec)—48 (54, 60, 64) sts.

Work 5 (5, 4, 4) rnds, repeat last 6 (6, 5, 5) rnds, 7 (5, 11, 5) times more.

Next rnd: k2tog, work around, end k2tog (2 st dec).

Work 4 (4, 3, 3) rnds, repeat last 5 (5, 4, 4) rnds, 2 (5, 1, 9) times more—28 (32, 34, 34) sts remain.

cuff
Work for 2"/5cm.

BO loosely.

Work second sleeve same as the first.

finishing
Sew underarms together and weave in ends.

basic heavy worsted pullover: 8 st gauge

instructions

collar (work ITR)

Using 16"/40cm cn, CO 64 (68, 72, 76) sts.

Work collar.

yoke (work ITR)

Place markers:

Rnd 1 (RS): k27 (29, 31, 33) front sts, pm, k9 sleeve sts, pm, k19 (21, 23, 25) back sts, pm, k9 sleeve sts, pm.

Rnd 2 *(Inc row)*: m1, *k to 1 st before marker, m1, sl m, m1, repeat from * around 3 times more, k until 1 st remains, m1 (8 sts inc)—72 (76, 80, 84) sts.

Rnd 3: k (sl markers along the way).

Repeat Rnds 2 and 3, 22 (25, 28, 31) times more—248 (276, 304, 332) sts.

divide yoke (work ITR)

Separate body and sleeve sts:

K73 (81, 89, 97) front sts, CO 2 sts, pm, CO 1 st, place 55 (61, 67, 73) sleeve sts on 16"/40cm cn and *hold aside*, k65 (73, 81, 89) back sts, CO 1 st, pm, CO 2 sts, place 55 (61, 67, 73) sleeve sts on 16"/40cm cn and *hold aside*—144 (160, 176, 173) body sts remain on main cn.

body (work ITR)

Join front and back portions, work for 11(12, 13, 14)"/28(31, 33, 36)cm.

hem

Work for 2"/5cm.

BO loosely.

sleeves (work ITR)

Work each sleeve separately, changing to dpn as necessary:

Using 55 (61, 67, 73) sts on 16"/40cm cn, CO 1 st, pm (underarm), CO 1 st—57 (63, 69, 75) sts.

Work for 1"/2.5cm.

Beg underarm sleeve dec:

Next rnd: k2tog, work around, end k2tog (2 sts dec)—55 (61, 67, 73) sts.

Work 4 (4, 3, 3) rnds, repeat last 5 (5, 4, 4) rnds, 7 (5, 14, 7) times more.

Next rnd: k2tog, work around, end k2tog (2 sts dec).

Work 3 (3, 0, 2) rnds, repeat last 4 (4, 0, 3) rnds, 3 (6, 0, 9) times more—33 (37, 39, 39) sts.

cuff

Work for 2"/5cm.

BO loosely. Work second sleeve same as the first.

finishing

Sew underarms together and weave in ends.

basic heavy worsted pullover: 10 st gauge

instructions

collar (work ITR)

Using 16"/40cm cn, CO 72 (76, 81, 84) sts.

Work collar.

yoke (work ITR)

Place markers:

Rnd 1 (RS): k31 (33, 36, 37) front sts, pm, k9 sleeve sts, pm, k23 (25, 27, 29) back sts, pm, k9 sleeve sts, pm.

Rnd 2 *(Inc row)*: m1, *k to 1 st before marker, m1, sl m, m1, repeat from * around 3 times more, k until 1 st remains, m1 (8 sts inc)—80 (84, 89, 92) sts.

Rnd 3: k (sl markers along the way).

Repeat Rnds 2 and 3, 25 (27, 31,34) times more—280 (300, 337, 364) sts.

divide yoke (work ITR)

Separate body and sleeve sts:
RS: k83 (89, 100, 107) front sts, CO 1 (2, 2, 2) sts, pm, CO 1 (2, 2, 2) sts, place 61 (65, 73, 79) sleeve sts on 16"/40cm cn and *hold aside,* k75 (81, 91, 99) back sts, CO 1 (2, 2, 2) sts, pm, CO 1 (2, 2, 2) st, place 61 (65, 73, 79) sleeve sts on 16"/40cm cn and *hold aside*—162 (178, 199, 214) body sts remain on main cn.

body (work ITR)

Work for 11 (12, 13, 14)"/28 (31, 33, 36)cm.

hem

Work for 2"/5cm.

BO loosely.

sleeves (work ITR)

Work sleeves separately, changing to dpn as necessary:
Using 61 (65, 73, 79) sts on 16"/40cm cn, CO 1 st, pm (underarm), CO 1 st—63 (67, 75, 81) sts.

Work for 1"/2.5cm.

Beg underarm sleeve dec:
Next rnd: k2tog, work around, end k2tog (2 sts dec).

Work 4 (5, 4, 3) rnds, repeat last 5 (6, 5, 4) rnds, 10 (0, 7, 15) times more.

Next rnd: k2tog, work around, end k2tog (2 sts dec)—61 (65, 73, 79) sts.

Work 3 (4, 3, 2) rnds, repeat last 4 (5, 4, 3) rnds, 1 (11, 6, 1) times more—37 (41, 45, 45) sts.

cuff

Work for 2"/5cm.

BO loosely.

Work second sleeve same as the first.

finishing

Sew underarms together and weave in ends.

---

basic heavy worsted cardigan: 8 st gauge

sizes
Small (Medium, Large, X-Large)

finished measurements
Bust 32–34 (36-38, 40-42, 44-46)"/81–86(92–97, 102–107, 112–117)cm

Garment 36 (40, 44, 48)"/91 (102, 112, 122)cm

materials
Yarn: 900(1000, 1200, 1400)yd/823 (915, 1098, 1281)m heavy worsted yarn

Needles: 5-5.5 mm (8-9 US) *or size to obtain gauge*

Circular (cn): one 29"/74cm, two 16"/41cm

Double-pointed (dpn): 10"/25cm set

4 stitch markers

Tapestry needle

gauge
16 sts/20 rows = 4"/10cm in St st
Always take time to check your gauge.

instructions

collar (work B&F)

Using 16"/40cm cn, CO 64 (68, 72, 76) sts.
Work collar.

yoke (work B&F)

Place markers:
Row 1 (RS): k11 (12, 13, 14) left front sts, pm, k9 sleeve sts, pm, k18 (20, 22, 24) back sts, pm, k9 sleeve sts, pm, k11 (12, 13, 14) right front sts.

Row 2(WS): p (sl markers along the way).

Row 3 *(Inc row):* *k to 1 st before next marker, m1, sl m, m1, repeat from * across 3 times more, k to end—72 (76, 80, 84) sts.

Repeat Rows 2 and 3, 22 (25, 28, 31) times more—248 (276, 304, 332) sts.

---

divide yoke (work B&F)

Separate body and sleeve sts:
RS: k37 (41, 45, 49) left front sts, CO 2 sts, pm, CO 1 st, place 55 (61, 67, 73) sleeve sts on 16"/40cm cn and *hold aside,* k65 (73, 81, 89) back sts, CO 1 st, pm, CO 2 sts, place 55 (61, 67, 73) sleeve sts on 16"/40cm cn and *hold aside,* k37 (41, 45, 49) right front sts—144 (160, 176, 192) body sts remain on main cn.

body (work B&F)

Join front and back portions, work for 11 (12, 13, 14)"/28 (31, 33, 36)cm.

hem

Work hem for 2"/5cm.

BO loosely.

sleeves (work ITR)

Work sleeves separately, changing to dpn necessary:
Using 55 (61, 67, 73) sts on 16"/40cm cn:
CO 1 st, pm (underarm), CO 1 st—57 (63, 69, 75) sts.

Work for 1"/2.5cm.

Beg underarm sleeve dec:
Next rnd: k2tog, work around, end k2tog (2 st dec)—55 (61, 65, 73) sts.

Work 4 (4, 3, 3) rnds, repeat last 5 (5, 4, 4) rnds, 7 (5, 14, 7) times more.

Next rnd: k2tog, work around, end k2tog (2 st dec).

Work 3 (3, 0, 2) rnds, repeat last 4 (4, 0, 3) rnds, 3 (6, 0, 9) times more—33 (37, 39, 39) sts.

cuff

Work cuff for 2"/5cm.

BO loosely.

Work second sleeve same as the first.

finishing

Sew underarms together and weave in ends.

basic heavy worsted cardigan: 10 st gauge

sizes
Small (Medium, Large, X-Large)

finished measurements
Bust 32–34 (36-38, 40-42, 44-46)"/81–86(92–97, 102–107, 112–117)cm

Garment 36 (40, 44, 48)"/91 (102, 112, 122)cm

materials
Yarn: 1000 (1200, 1300, 1500)yd/915 (1098, 1189, 1372)m heavy worsted yarn

Needles: 5-5.5 mm (8-9 US) *or size to obtain gauge*

Circular (cn): one 29"/74cm, two 16"/41cm *or size to obtain gauge*

Double-pointed (dpn): 10"/25cm set

4 stitch markers

Tapestry needle

gauge
18 sts/22rows = 4"/10cm

Always take time to check your gauge.

instructions

collar (work B&F)
Using 16"/40cm cn, CO 72 (76, 81, 84) sts.

Work collar.

yoke (work B&F)
Row 1 (RS): k13 (14, 15, 16) left front sts, pm, k9 sleeve sts, pm, k22 (24, 27, 28) back sts, pm, k9 sleeve sts, pm, k13 (14, 15, 16) right front sts.

Row 2 (WS): p (sl markers along the way).

Row 3 *(Inc row)*: *k to 1 st before next marker, m1, sl m, m1, repeat from * across 3 times more, k to end—80 (84, 89, 92) sts.

Repeat Rows 2 and 3, 25 (27, 31, 34) times more—280 (300, 337, 364) sts.

divide yoke (work B&F)
Separate body and sleeve sts:
RS: k42 (45, 50, 54) left front sts, CO 1 (2, 2, 2) sts, pm, CO 1 (2, 2, 2) sts, place 61 (65, 73, 79) sleeve sts on 16"/40cm cn and *hold aside*, k75 (81, 91, 99) back sts, CO 1 (2, 2, 2) sts, pm, CO 1 (2, 2, 2) sts, place 61 (65, 73, 79) sleeve sts on 16"/40cm cn and *hold aside*, k42 (45, 50, 54) right front sts— 162 (178, 199, 214) body sts remain on main cn.

body (work B&F)
Work body for 11 (12, 13, 14)"/28 (31, 33, 36)cm.

hem
Work hem for 2"/5cm.

BO loosely.

sleeves (work ITR)
Work sleeves separately, changing to dpn as necessary:
Using 61 (65, 73, 79) sts on 16"/40cm cn, CO 1 st, pm (underarm):

CO 1 st—63 (67, 75, 81) sts.

Work for 1"/2.5cm.

Beg underarm sleeve dec:
Next rnd: k2tog, work around, end k2tog (2 st dec)—61 (65, 73, 79) sts.

Work 4 (5, 4, 3) rnds, repeat last 5 (6, 5, 4) rnds, 10 (0, 7, 15) times more.

Next rnd: k2tog, work around, end k2tog (2 st dec).

Work 3 (4, 3, 2) rnds, repeat last 4 (5, 4, 3) rnds, 1 (11, 6, 1) times more—37 (41, 45, 45) sts.

cuff
Work cuff for 2"/5cm.

BO loosely.

Work second sleeve same as the first.

finishing
Sew underarms together and weave in ends.

---

basic dk pullover: 8 st gauge

sizes
Small (Medium, Large, X-Large)

finished measurements
Bust 32–34 (36-38, 40-42, 44-46)"/81–86(92–97, 102–107, 112–117)cm

Garment 36 (40, 44, 48)"/91 (102, 112, 122)cm

materials
Yarn: 1300 (1500, 1700, 1800)yd/1189(1372,1555,1647)m dk weight yarn

Needles: 3.75-4.5mm (5-7 US) *or size to obtain gauge*

Circular (cn): one 29"/74cm, two 16"/41cm *or size to obtain gauge*

Double-pointed (dpn): 10"/25cm set

4 stitch markers

Tapestry needle

gauge
20 sts/24 rows = 4"/10cm

Always take time to check your gauge.

instructions

collar (work ITR)
Using 16"/40cm cn, CO 80 (85, 90, 95) sts.

Work collar.

yoke (work ITR)
Place markers:
Rnd 1 (RS): k35 (38, 40, 43) front sts, pm, k10 sleeve sts, pm, k25 (27, 30, 32) back sts, pm, k10 sleeve sts, pm.

Rnd 2 *(Inc row)*: m1, *k to 1 st before marker, m1, sl m, m1, repeat from * around 3 times more, k until 1 st remains, m1 (8 sts inc)—88 (93, 98, 103) sts.

Rnd 3: k (sl markers along the way).

Repeat Rnds 2 and 3, 27 (30, 34, 37) times more—304 (333, 370, 399) sts.

divide yoke (work ITR)

Separate body and sleeve sts:

RS: k91 (100, 110, 119) front sts, CO 2 (2, 2, 3) sts, pm, CO 2 (2, 2, 3) sts, place 66 (72, 80, 86) sleeve sts on 16"/40cm cn and *hold aside*, k81 (89, 100, 108) back sts, CO 2 (2, 2, 3) sts, pm, CO 2 (2, 2, 3) sts, place 66 (72, 80, 86) sleeve sts on 16"/40cm cn and *hold aside*—180 (197, 218, 239) body sts remain on main cn.

body (work ITR)

Join front and back, work for 11 (12, 13, 14)"/28 (31, 33, 36)cm.

hem

Work for 2"/5cm.

BO loosely.

sleeves (work ITR)

Work sleeves separately, changing to dpn as necessary:

Using 66 (72, 80, 86) sts on 16"/40cm cn, CO 1 st, pm (underarm), CO 1 st—68 (74, 82, 88) sts.

Work for 1"/2.5cm.

Beg underarm sleeve dec:
Next rnd: k2tog, work around, end k2tog (2 sts dec)—66 (72, 80, 86) sts.

Work 8 (8, 8, 6) rnds, repeat last 9 (9, 9, 7) rnds, 3 (6, 1, 8) times more.

Next rnd: k2tog, work around, end k2tog (2 sts dec).

Work 7 (7, 7, 5) rnds, repeat last 8 (1, 8, 6) rnds, 5 (2, 8, 4) times—48 (54, 60, 60) sts.

cuff

Work for 2"/5cm.

BO loosely

Work second sleeve same as the first.

finishing

Sew underarms together and weave in ends.

---

basic dk pullover: 10 st gauge

sizes
Small (Medium, Large, X-Large)

finished measurements
Bust 32–34 (36-38, 40-42, 44-46)"/81–86(92–97, 102–107, 112–117)cm

Garment 36 (40, 44, 48)"/91 (102, 112, 122)cm

materials
Yarn: 1400 (1600, 1800, 2000)yd/1281(1464, 1647, 1830)m dk weight yarn

Needles: 3.75-4.5mm (5-7 US) *or size to obtain gauge*

Circular (cn): one 29"/74cm, two 16"/41cm *or size to obtain gauge*

Double-pointed (dpn): 10"/25cm set

4 stitch markers

Tapestry needle

gauge
22 sts/26 rows = 4"/10cm

Always take time to check your gauge.

instructions

collar (work ITR)

Using 16"/40cm cn, CO 88 (93, 99, 104) sts.

Work collar.

yoke (work ITR)

Place markers:
Rnd 1 (RS): k39 (42, 45, 47) front sts, pm, k10 sleeve sts, pm, k29 (31, 34, 37) back sts, pm, k10 sleeve sts, pm.

Rnd 2 (Inc row): m1, *k to 1 st before marker, m1, sl m, m1, repeat from * around 3 times more, k until 1 st remains, m1 (8 sts inc)—96 (101, 107, 112) sts.

Rnd 3: k (sl markers along the way).

Repeat Rnds 2 and 3, 29 (33 37, 40) times more—328 (365, 403, 432) sts.

---

divide yoke (work ITR)

Separate body and sleeve sts:

RS: k99 (110, 121, 129) front sts, CO 2 (2, 2, 3) sts, pm, CO 2 (2, 2 ,3) sts, place 70 (78, 86, 92) sleeve sts on 16"/40cm cn and *hold aside*, k89 (99, 110, 119) back sts, CO 2 (2, 2, 3) sts, pm, CO 2 (2, 2, 3) sts, place 70 (78, 86, 92) sleeve sts on 16"/40cm cn and *hold aside*—196 (217, 239, 260) body sts remain on main cn.

body (work ITR)

Join front and back portions, work for 11 (12, 13, 14)"/28 (31, 33, 35)cm.

hem

Work for 2"/5cm.

BO loosely.

sleeves (work ITR)

Work sleeves separately, changing to dpn as necessary:

Using 70 (78, 86, 92) sts on16"/40cm cn, CO 2 sts at underarm, pm between—72 (80, 88, 94) sts.

Work for 1"/2.5cm.

Beg underarm sleeve dec:
K2tog, work around, end k2tog (2 sts dec)—70 (78, 86, 92) sts.

Work 9 (9, 8, 7) rnds, repeat last 10 (10, 9, 8) rnds, 0 (3, 9, 2) times more.

K2tog, work around, end k2tog (2 sts dec).

Work 8 (8, 7, 6) rnds, repeat last 9 (9, 8, 7) rnds, 8 (5, 0, 10) times more—52 (60, 66, 66) sts.

cuff

Work for 2"/5cm.

BO loosely.

Work second sleeve same as the first.

finishing

Sew underarms together and weave in ends.

basic dk cardigan: 8 st gauge

sizes
Small (Medium, Large, X-Large)

finished measurements
Bust 32–34 (36-38, 40-42, 44-46)"/81–86(92–97, 102–107, 112–117)cm

Garment 36 (40, 44, 48)"/91 (102, 112, 122)cm

materials
Yarn: 1300(1500, 1700, 1800)yd/1189(1372, 1555, 1647)m dk weight yarn

Needles: 3.75 - 4.5mm (5-7 US) or size to obtain gauge

Circular (cn): one 29"/74cm, two 16"/41cm or size to obtain gauge

Double-pointed (dpn): 10"/25cm set

4 stitch markers

Tapestry needle

gauge
20 sts/24 rows = 4"/10cm in St st

Always take time to check your gauge.

instructions

collar (work B&F)
Using 16"/40cm cn, CO 80 (85, 90, 95) sts.

Work collar.

yoke (work B&F)
Row 1 (RS): k17 (19, 20, 21) left front sts, pm, k10 sleeve sts, pm, k24 (27, 30, 33) back sts, pm, k10 sleeve sts, pm, k17 (19, 20, 21) right front sts.

Row 2 (WS): p (sl markers along the way).

Row 3 (Inc row): *k to 1 st before next marker, m1, sl m, m1, repeat from * across 3 times more, k to end—88 (93, 98, 103) sts.

Repeat Rows 2 and 3, 27 (30, 34, 37) times more—304 (333, 370, 399) sts.

divide yoke (work B&F)
Separate body and sleeve sts:

RS: k46 (50, 55, 59) left front sts, CO 2 (2, 2, 3) sts, pm, CO 2 (2, 2, 3) sts, place 66 (72, 80, 86) sleeve sts on 16"/40cm cn and *hold aside*, k80 (89, 100, 109) back sts, CO 2 (2, 2, 3) sts, pm, CO 2 (2, 2, 3) sts, place 66 (72, 80, 86) sleeve sts on 16"/40cm cn and *hold aside*, k46 (50, 55, 59) right front sts—180 (197, 218, 239) sts remain on main cn.

body (work B&F)
Work for 11 (12, 13, 14)"/28 (31, 33, 36)cm.

hem
Work for 2"/5cm.

BO loosely.

sleeves (work ITR)
Work sleeves separately, changing to dpn as needed:

Using 66 (72, 80, 86) sts on 16"/40cm cn, CO 1 st, pm (underarm), CO 1 st—68 (74, 82, 88) sts.

Work for 1"/2.5cm

Beg underarm sleeve dec:

Next rnd: k2tog, work around, end k2tog (2 st dec)—66 (72, 80, 85) sts.

Work 8 (8, 8, 6) rnds, repeat last 9 (9, 9, 7) rnds, 3 (6, 1, 8) times more.

Next rnd: k2tog, work around, end k2tog (2 st dec).

Work 7 (7, 7, 5) rnds, repeat last 8 (1, 8, 6) rnds, 5 (2, 8, 4) times more—48 (54, 60, 60) sts.

cuff
Work for 2"/5cm.

BO loosely.

Work second sleeve same as the first.

finishing
Sew underarms together and weave in ends.

basic dk cardigan: 10 st gauge

sizes
Small (Medium, Large, X-Large)

finished measurements
Bust 32–34 (36-38, 40-42, 44-46)"/81–86(92–97, 102–107, 112–117)cm

Garment 36 (40, 44, 48)"/91 (102, 112, 122)cm

materials
Yarn: 1400(1600, 1800, 2000) yd/1281(1464, 1647, 1830)m dk weight yarn

Needles: 3.75 - 4.5mm (5-7 US) or size to obtain gauge

Circular (cn): one 29"/74cm, two 16"/41cm or size to obtain gauge

Double-pointed (dpn): 10"/25cm set

4 stitch markers

Tapestry needle

gauge
22 sts/26 rows = 4"/10cm

Always take time to check your gauge.

instructions

collar (work B&F)
Using 16"/40cm cn, CO 88 (93, 99, 104) sts.

Work collar.

yoke (work B&F)
Row 1 (RS): k19 (21,22, 23) left front sts, pm, k10 sleeve sts, pm, k30 (31, 35, 38) back sts, pm, k10 sleeve sts, pm, k19(19, 21, 22, 23) right front sts.

Row 2 (WS): p (sl markers along the way).

Row 3 (Inc row): *k to 1 st before next marker, m1, sl m, m1, repeat from * across 3 times more, k to end—96 (101, 107, 112) sts.

Repeat Rows 2 and 3, 29 (33, 37, 40) times more—328 (365, 403, 432) sts.

divide yoke (work B&F)

Separate body and sleeve sts:
RS: k49 (55, 60, 64) left front sts, CO 2 (2, 2, 3) sts, pm, CO 2 (2, 2, 3) sts, place 70 (78, 86, 92) sleeve sts on 16"/40cm cn and *hold aside,* k90 (99, 111, 120) back sts, CO 2 (2, 2, 3) sts, pm, CO 2 (2, 2, 3) sts, place 70 (78, 86, 92) sleeve sts on 16"/40cm cn and *hold aside,* k49 (55, 60, 64) right front sts—196 (217, 239, 260) body sts remain on main cn.

body (work B&F)

Work body for 11(12, 13, 14)"/28 (31, 33, 36)cm.

hem

Work for 2"/5cm.

BO loosely.

sleeves (work ITR)

Work sleeve separately, changing to dpn as necessary
Using 70 (78, 86, 92) sts on 16"/40cm cn, CO 1 st, pm (underarm), CO 1 st—72 (80, 88, 94) sts.

Work for 1"/2.5cm.

Beg underarm sleeve dec:
Next rnd: k2tog, work around, end k2tog (2 st dec)—70 (78, 86, 92) sts.

Work 9 (9, 8, 7) rnds, repeat last 10 (10, 9, 8) rnds, 0 (3, 9, 2) times more.

Next rnd: k2tog, work around, end k2tog (2 st dec).

Work 8 (8, 7, 6) rnds, repeat last 9 (9, 8, 7) rnds, 8 (5, 0, 10) times more—52 (60, 66, 66) sts.

cuff

Work for 2"/5cm.

BO loosely.

Work second sleeve same as the first.

finishing

Sew underarms together and weave in ends.

METRIC CONVERSION CHART

INCHES	METRIC (MM/CM)	INCHES	METRIC (MM/CM)	INCHES	METRIC (MM/CM)
1/8	3 mm	8 1/2	21.6 cm	23	58.4 cm
3/16	5 mm	9	22.9 cm	23 1/2	59.7 cm
1/4	6 mm	9 1/2	24.1 cm	24	61 cm
5/16	8 mm	10	25.4 cm	24 1/2	62.2 cm
3/8	9.5 mm	10 1/2	26.7 cm	25	63.5 cm
7/16	1.1 cm	11	27.9 cm	25 1/2	64.8 cm
1/2	1.3 cm	11 1/2	29.2 cm	26	66 cm
9/16	1.4 cm	12	30.5 cm	26 1/2	67.3 cm
5/8	1.6 cm	12 1/2	31.8 cm	27	68.6 cm
11/16	1.7 cm	13	33 cm	27 1/2	69.9 cm
3/4	1.9 cm	13 1/2	34.3 cm	28	71.1 cm
13/16	2.1 cm	14	35.6 cm	28 1/2	72.4 cm
7/8	2.2 cm	14 1/2	36.8 cm	29	73.7 cm
15/16	2.4 cm	15	38.1 cm	29 1/2	74.9 cm
1	2.5 cm	15 1/2	39.4 cm	30	76.2 cm
1 1/2	3.8 cm	16	40.6 cm	30 1/2	77.5 cm
2	5 cm	16 1/2	41.9 cm	31	78.7 cm
2 1/2	6.4 cm	17	43.2 cm	31 1/2	80 cm
3	7.6 cm	17 1/2	44.5 cm	32	81.3 cm
3 1/2	8.9 cm	18	45.7 cm	32 1/2	82.6 cm
4	10.2 cm	18 1/2	47 cm	33	83.8 cm
4 1/2	11.4 cm	19	48.3 cm	33 1/2	85 cm
5	12.7 cm	19 1/2	49.5 cm	34	86.4 cm
5 1/2	14 cm	20	50.8 cm	34 1/2	87.6 cm
6	15.2 cm	20 1/2	52 cm	35	88.9 cm
6 1/2	16.5 cm	21	53.3 cm	35 1/2	90.2 cm
7	17.8 cm	21 1/2	54.6 cm	36	91.4 cm
7 1/2	19 cm	22	55 cm	36 1/2	92.7 cm
8	20.3 cm	22 1/2	57.2 cm	37	94.0 cm

ABBREVIATIONS & KNITTING TERMINOLOGY

beg	beginning
B&F	back-and-forth
BO	bind off
CO	cast on
cont	continue
cn	circular needle
dec	decrease
dpn	double-pointed needle(s)
inc	increase
ITR	in-the-round
k	knit
KB	knit st with a bead
K2tog	knit two stitches together
MB	make a bobble
m1	increase by knitting into the back of a stitch and then knitting the stitch itself
p	purl
p2tog	purl two stitches together
pm	place marker
psso	pass slip st over
r	row
rnd	round
RS	right side
SH	stitch-holder
sl1	slip a stitch
slm	slip marker
sn	straight needle
ST.st.	stockingnette stitch; (B&F) alternating knit and purl rows, (ITR) knit every rnd
t1	increase by pulling up a stitch from between the two stitches in the row below
WS	wrong side
YO	yarn over

Notes on Suppliers

Usually, the supplies you need for making the projects in Lark books can be found at your local craft supply store, discount mart, home improvement center, or retail shop relevant to the topic of the book. Occasionally, however, you may need to buy materials or tools from specialty suppliers. In order to provide you with the most up-to-date information, we have created a list of suppliers on our website, which we update on a regular basis. Visit us at www.larkbooks.com, click on "Craft Supply Sources," and then click on the relevant topic. You will find numerous companies listed with their web address and/or mailing address and phone number.

About the Author

Cathy Carron is a knitwear designer and owner of PondEdge/cathy carron, a knit hat business based in New York and Connecticut. She is the author of *Hip Knit Hats* (Lark, 2005), and has been a contributor to *Vogue-On-the-Go: Bags & Purses* (Vogue 2006), *Classic Elite Patterns*, and *The Michael's Book of Needlecrafts* (Lark, 2005). She lives in New York City with her husband and two daughters. More of her work can be seen at her website www.pondedge.net.

Acknowledgments

Many thanks to the following for their kind attention and promptness in providing yarns and materials for this book:

Susan Mills at JCA/Reynolds

Doris Erb at Bernat

Deanna Gavioli at Berroco

Linda Niemeyer at Blue Sky, Alpacas

Judy Croucher at Classic Elite

Arthur Karapetyan at Karabella

Stephanie Klose at Lionbrand

Cristina Hyde at Muench

Jessica Oas at Rowan

Ketsia Poteau at MJ Trimming

Index